The Lame Shall T
How a One-Legged Missionary Transformed China

By Grace Stott

Contributed by Eugene Bach & Bethany Hope

The content of this book was produced using writings in the public domain, namely *Twenty-Six Years of Missionary Work in China* by Grace Stott. The content has been partially modified for a modern audience.

The Lame Shall Take the Prey: How a One-Legged Missionary Transformed China

By Grace Stott

Contributed by Eugene Bach & Bethany Hope

Published by Underground Publishing House LTD

20-22 Wenlock Road

London, N1 7GU

info@undergroundpublishing.co.uk

ISBN: 9798850618506

THE LAME SHALL TAKE THE PREY: HOW A ONE-LEGGED MISSIONARY TRANSFORMED CHINA

GRACE STOTT *OF THE CHINA INLAND MISSION*

In the heart of our London Publishing House, the contents of this book were crafted from the public domain with the goal of edifying and educating a new generation with the voices of old. Though most of the writings are left in their original state, some things have been changed and tailored to be better understood by a more modern audience.

To breathe life into literature, both neglected and forbidden, is our life and passion.

It has been said, "books do not age as you and I do. They will speak still when you and I are gone, to generations we will never see. Yes, the books must survive."[1] Even in places where voices have been banished to the underground, the books must survive.

---

[1] Corrie ten Boom, *The Hiding Place: The Triumphant True Story of Corrie ten Boom* (1971)

Table of Contents

INTRODUCTION

The rebirth of this book happened when stumbling across a small brittle letter from the mid-1800s. The paper was worn and stained, the handwritten old English barely legible, but the fragile correspondence was a hidden treasure that had been tucked away and concealed from human eyes for over a hundred years. Sitting in a quiet dusty library in Cambridge University was a single piece of paper that changed the entire history of China forever.

It was a letter from Cambridge University, rejecting the application of George Stott.

This blow of rejection led Stott to refocus his life to China, going on to become the first foreign missionary to ever set foot in the city of Wenzhou, China.

He was not the missionary society's first choice; at nineteen his leg was amputated and he went through life with a wooden leg. In the mid-1800s, traveling through China with only one leg was just shy of impossible. When the legendary Hudson Taylor asked Stott why he was going to China with only one leg, he confidently and without desire for pity replied, "I do not see those with two legs going, so I must."

George and his wife, Grace Stott, were the very first pioneer missionaries to bring the Gospel to Wenzhou, which is now known as the "Jerusalem of China," because of its large and thriving Christian population. This book, written by Grace Stott herself, tells the untold story of how God used the most unlikely individuals to transform a city which impacted a nation that, today, is experiencing the world's largest revival.

Their journey to China was anything but easy and the joys and pains of their 26-year journey are carefully captured in the following pages.

Rejected, attacked, persecuted, chased, stoned, and at one point even accused of cutting the hearts and liver from small Chinese children to grind up into medicine, George and Grace Stott did not stop preaching the Gospel. George, the one-legged Scotsman, limped from village to village preaching the Good News of Jesus Christ. In his own words: “the lame shall take the prey.”

Before George and Grace arrived in China, Wenzhou was a remote port city, known to have more idol worship than any other in China. When they departed China however, they had planted three churches with over three hundred Christians who were all pastored by indigenous Chinese pastors. This feat was simply unheard of in the China of the 1800s.

And today? The massive metropolitan of Wenzhou has more ethnic Christians than any other city in China, with an average of one church for every square kilometre. There are so many powerful church movements there that we dedicated a special chapter to it in our book, THE UNDERGROUND CHURCH.

The words in this book do not read like any modern writing that the reader might be accustomed to. Prepare to be accosted by forgotten mission concepts and ideas that can only be found in the pages of raw missionary writings from over 150 years ago. Don't be intimidated by the outdated vocabulary, but instead let this century-old language transport you to another place and time.

Finally, and above all, let the reader permit himself to bleed as the Sword of the Spirit wrapped in the dense theological and emotional presentation of this forgotten work cuts deep into his fleshly understanding of the Word. May the mind and soul be forever transformed, chasing the legacy of those who have gone before us. "Follow my example, as I follow the example of Christ." 1 Corinthians 1:11

- Underground

PREFACE

The work of God recorded in these pages is no longer an experiment, and it is well that Mrs. Stott has been able, during her furlough, to put in more permanent form some of the incidents which many of us have heard with deepest interest from her own lips in missionary meetings, or on more private occasions.

It has been my privilege to be acquainted with this work from its commencement. With earnest prayer I commended Mr. Stott to God for his difficult journey, for in those times Wenzhou was not a free port, and the eight days overland travel through unknown and mountainous country would have been somewhat formidable for a good walker, while for one on crutches it was much more so. He left Scotland, however, believing that "the lame should take the prey," and he was spared to do so to no small extent.

I had visited Mr. Stott during his early labours there, and seen how much he needed domestic help, and how handicapped he was in the charge of his boys' boarding-school, before I had the pleasure of welcoming Miss Ciggie (whom I had known in Glasgow) on her arrival in China, twenty-six years ago, to become his wife.

Having closely followed the progress of the work through these twenty-five years, and having paid my last visits to Wenzhou since Mrs. Stott left, it was with special interest and pleasure that I snatched time to read most of her manuscript. It is emphatically a story of work-earnest, persevering work which God has blessed: an unvarnished account, it brings out clearly the lights and shades of missionary service.

I did not find one dull paragraph. Those who begin to read the book will want to finish it, and it cannot fail to be a blessing to the reader.

It is an unfinished record, and, since Mrs. Stott asked me to write a few lines of preface, a joyful letter from Miss Christabel Williams tells of the conversion of sixteen of the twenty-six girls in the boarding-school: four of the children were previously converted, and several of the remaining six-the little ones of the school-were seeking the Lord.

May many readers be led to pray for the work and workers in Wenzhou!

J. Hudson Tayor

CHINA INLAND MISSION,

NEWINGTON GREEN,

LONDON, N.

January, 1897.

CHAPTER 1

Follow Me

Follow Me, and I will make you fishers of men." Matthew 4:19

My first interest in China began in the spring of 1865 when Mr. Hudson Taylor, accompanied by Mr. (now Dr.) Barchet and his companion, visited Glasgow. The two latter were *en route* for China, sailing in a few days and Mr. Taylor had come to wish them good-bye and God-speed. They addressed a small meeting, and as I listened to Mr. Taylor's tale of the darkness of China and the terrible need of workers there, there came a question that would be answered, "Why may you not go to tell of a Saviour's love?"

I had been converted four years, and had begun in a feeble way to serve the Lord who had bought me, at first by tract distribution, then Sunday-school teaching. The Lord had often also graciously used me to lead many an anxious soul into the light, but up to this time I had never thought of mission work, never supposed I had any call beyond my native city of Glasgow.

For days this question kept ringing in my heart. I had no home ties, it was true; but was I fit? Then, too, at that time I had never heard of a young girl going to a heathen land - was it practicable? This latter question I decided to ask Mr. Taylor. He saw no reason why I should not go, even though but twenty years of age, if called of God, and if called, surely the fitness would be given by Him.

After much prayer and consideration, Mr. Taylor invited me to go to London, that by mutual prayer and knowledge of one another, God's way might be made clear. I arrived just the day before Mr. and Mrs. Stevenson's marriage. They and Mr. Stott, whom I then met for the first time, sailed three weeks afterwards for China.

Mr. Stott had been brought up to farm work, but when he was about nineteen years of age he slipped on the road and knocked his knee against a stone. This simple accident resulted in white swelling, which, two years later, necessitated the amputation of the left leg. For nine months he lay a helpless invalid, and it was during this time that the Lord graciously saved his soul. So far he had been careless and indifferent to the love of God in Christ Jesus, but now, in his helpless condition, and what seemed his ruined future, how precious that love became! After his recovery he began to teach in a school, and had been thus employed several years when he first heard of China's needs through a friend, who himself was going out.

In accepting Mr. Stott for mission work, Mr. Taylor manifested that faith which has so eminently characterised him, for surely no Society would have sent a lame man to such a country to pioneer work, and Mr. Stott often referred with gratitude to Mr. Taylor's acceptance of him. When asked why he, with only one leg, should think of going to China, his remark was, "I do not see those with two legs going, so I must." As I saw them slowly sail out of the docks, a great hope welled up in my heart that I should soon follow, though at that time I little thought that my life and work would be blended with his.

When asked why he, with only one leg, should think of going to China, his remark was, "I do not see those with two legs going, so I must."

I continued in London a few months, when it was definitely settled that I should accompany Mr. and Mrs. Taylor and party, who were to sail the following May.

Almost as soon as that decision was arrived at my health began to give way, though up to that time I scarce remember one day of sickness. After trying several places, with the vain hope my illness might prove a temporary weakness, and that I might still be able to go forward, the doctors gave it as their definite decision that I ought not to go to China at present.

Mr. Taylor reluctantly communicated this decision to me, but added, "I hope you will be able to follow us in a year." This news was a great blow to me; I had thought I was willing, for God's will only, that I would be content to go or stay, just as He called; but when the word came "stay" I was bitterly disappointed.

This led to much heart searching: for the first time I saw how easy it was to deceive oneself, and night after night I cried to God to save me from self-deception.

One night, when on my knees, with tearful confession of self-will, it seemed as if I heard a voice saying, "If you still want to serve me go back to Glasgow, and take my messages to the Salt Market and the district round about."

My heart almost stood still: the Salt Market was one of the vilest and most wicked places in Glasgow, inhabited almost exclusively by thieves and women of ill-repute. It was hardly fit for a man to go into such a place - could it be God was sending a young girl there, uncalled by man, unprotected, and without means of support - could that be God's will for me?

I knelt in silence; I dare not speak. I had had one lesson in self-will, and dared not say "No," while I feared to say "Yes." At last the answer came, "Yes, Lord; if Thou wilt go with me every step of the way." I then told the Lord that as I could not go alone I should refuse to go any day I did not feel His presence and power with me. From that hour strength seemed slowly to return. Meantime arrangements were being made for the sailing of the *Lammermuir* party. I offered to remain a few weeks and help with the outfits.

About a fortnight before the ship sailed, one of the party withdrew through the illness of her mother. Passages had been paid, and µnless another took her place the money would be lost. Mr. Taylor turned to me: I had been getting stronger - was it not possible that God, having made me willing to stay, was now opening the way for me to go?

To Mr. Taylor it almost appeared so.

I prayed, but could get no light; it seemed as if the Lord, having given me His orders, would hear nothing more on the subject, so I had to say, "I can't go," even though it almost broke my heart to say the word.

The *Lammermuir* sailed on May 26, 1866, and as I watched her towed slowly out from the docks I felt China must be left behind for the present. Mr. Taylor's home was broken up the day they left, but friends had kindly invited me to spend a few days with them previous to returning to Glasgow, and it was here I had my first lesson in faith.

The friend who had been as a mother to me after my grandmother's death had died during my stay in London. I had, therefore, no home to return to. I had paid all my incidental personal expenses, and never having referred to money matters, friends must have supposed I had plenty, but in fact I only had just enough to take me by rail to Glasgow.

Wishing to have a few shillings in my pocket, by which to obtain lodgings, I wanted to go by steamer, that being the cheaper way. Friends tried to dissuade me, not knowing my reason; the expenses were figured up and after removal of luggage, etc, I found I would save but four shillings and sixpence, and they urged it was not worth taking so long a journey for that sum.

I had been asked to visit a young lady on that day, and was about to write a note to say that, leaving by steamer, I could not keep my engagement, when the thought came to me, could I not give up that four shillings and sixpence for the Lord's sake?

Perhaps He had some service for me to do, or I might interest her in China, so I decided to go by the night train and keep my engagement. We had a time of sweet fellowship together, and, when leaving, she pressed a small packet into my hand, saying, "Take this as from Him." When I opened it, there was exactly four shillings and six pence inside!

Oh, how strengthened and helped I was by that simple act! It seemed as if God had said, "Do not doubt; I will care for you."

I had never heard of living by faith, and if asked could hardly have told the meaning of the words; but I did know if an earthly master sent his servant to do some special work for him, he would at least see that he had enough to eat, and I dared not think my heavenly Father would treat His child worse than that, so I was "without carefulness" in this matter.

I had learned to use my needle well, and thought I might help to support myself in that way. Having some warm Christian friends, I had no doubt that if I told them I wanted needlework they would be sure to let me have some, and for the rest the Lord would provide. My business was to do His will.

On my return to Glasgow I was still far from strong, but gave from ten till two daily in visiting the poor degraded outcasts of Salt Market district. No needlework offered, my Father seeing I was too weak to do anything more than the daily visiting. I soon learned why God had sent me in this way, for almost the first questions fiercely asked were: "What Church has sent you here?"

"No Church." "Who has sent you?"

"No one."

"Are you not paid for coming?"

"No."

"Then why do you come?"

"Because I love you; I have been saved myself, and I want you to be saved too." And when they found that I was not only willing to read with and pray for them, but to nurse poor sick ones, kindle a fire, make beef tea, or sweep a hearth if need be, beside nursing their babies, both hearts and homes were opened to me at once.

At first, the elders of the Church to which I belonged were uneasy at so young a girl going into dens of such wretchedness, and one elderly man warned me of the dangers to which I was exposing myself, and feared that evil might befall me; but I felt that was God's business.

He had sent me, and He was responsible, and never during the three and a half years I laboured amongst them did I receive the least insult or hear unbecoming language if they knew I was present.

After three months, during which time God had provided for all my wants in a remarkable manner, sending money from whence I did not know, so that I had lacked nothing, I was one day asked to speak with a few of the elders. They said they thought perhaps God had called me, and they would like a share in the work - would I accept a small sum from them weekly?

I told them I could not be put under any rule whatever; I had to feel my way to depend on God for wisdom by the hour, and must work just when and how I could; that if their money would mean being under their control, I must decline; but if they would like to help, no matter in how small a sum, leaving me quite free, I would rejoice in their fellowship.

From that hour, until I left for China, three and a half years afterwards, they stood by me, helping me on, but never interfering. In this way the Lord supplied all my wants.

It was not long before I began to see that I was the one God wanted to train through these means. I had all my life had a hatred and dread of sin and sinners. A bad person filled me with disgust, and it was not till I was sent down there among the utterly lost that I began to separate between sin and the sinner, and while hating the one to love the other.

It was not till I was sent out among the utterly lost that I began to separate between sin and the sinner, and while hating the one to love the other.

They had human hearts, and readily responded to the touch of love, and I felt circumstances and God's grace alone had made me to differ.

During that time, so far as I knew, only two had been converted, but God had put His child into His own school, and He was teaching her lessons that would have to be lived out when He gave her her life's work. Never, never shall I cease to give God thanks for those years of contact with sin and for the faith lessons learned there, yet during all the time I never once lost the consciousness that my life's work lay in China, and I had but to wait His time.

CHAPTER 2

In Due Season

In due season we shall reap, if we faint not." Galatians 6:9

In the meantime, Mr. Stott had, after eighteen months spent in the neighbourhood of Ningbo, acquiring that dialect, gone to Wenzhou, arriving there in November, 1867. He met with but scant courtesy.

For three months he and Mr. Jackson, who had accompanied him from Taizhou, lived in an inn. All feared them, and no one would rent a house to the hated foreigner. Again and again negotiations were almost complete, when the money would be returned and the weary search begin again.

At last a man of some influence, who had brought himself to despair by opium-smoking and gambling, offered a house, and was bold enough to brave all the consequences. Mr. Stott moved there as quietly as possible, but next day the news had spread, and a large angry crowd assembled, determined to turn him out. They battered in the gate, bent on mischief.

Mr. Stott came out and stood before them, and said, "You see I am a lame man; if I wanted to run away from you I could not; if you kill me you will, perhaps, get into trouble; if you let me alone you will find I shall do no harm; anyhow, I have come and mean to stay." They were taken aback by his quiet, strong words, and contenting themselves by throwing a few stones they dispersed and left him in peace.

As soon as possible he tried to begin a boys' school, and thought to induce regular attendance by providing them with a mid-day meal. A fair number attended, and they seemed to have made a good start, when one day, going into the schoolroom, he found the teacher, but no boys.

He asked the meaning of it all, and was told that a report had spread abroad that he was luring children in on purpose to take out their hearts and liver to compound into medicine, and their parents were afraid to expose their children to such terrible dangers. No respectable person would take the position of servant, and so weary months had to be passed alone, in the midst of many dangers and discomforts, before confidence was fairly won.

A report had spread that Mr. Stott was luring children in on purpose to take out their hearts and liver to compound into medicine, and the Chinese parents were afraid to expose their children to such terrible dangers.

Over two years he laboured alone and for more than a year of that time never saw an English face, or ever heard a word of the English language, for from the time he arrived in Wenzhou, in November, 1867, until he left, in February, 1870, to meet me, he had never left the city for a single night.

By that time he had established his boys' boarding school and had twelve boys entirely under his care; but only two men in the city had been baptized, and they proved disappointments in later years.

How much of his time was spent during these two years is given in a letter to a friend, written in 1869. He says, "My household consists of twelve boys, schoolmaster, my own teacher, two servant men, and an old washerwoman: if I rule them as I ought, it is well, but that is an open question. I shall give you a short account of how I spend my time.

Getting up in the morning at six o'clock, meditation, prayer, and breakfast over, I have a short lecture or exposition in the school, and prayers; then the needs of the family have to be examined and provided for, such as buying rice, vegetables, fish and firewood, needles, buttons, shoes, etc, the size, number, quality of each having to be decided upon. Marketing done, I go to my study, and prepare discourses for Sundays and evenings, or attend to any important visitor, ever seeking an opportunity of telling him of the true God, of sin, and salvation. After dinner I resume study, receive visitors, or ride out in the country, taking with me a few tracts, and find an opportunity to speak a word for Christ Jesus, for I dare not yet venture to preach in the streets.

By the time I get home the boys are out of school, and then I have to keep them busy and out of mischief till supper-time, which takes place after dark. This over, we have some recreation, recital of some tale from memory, or exhibition of pictures, with some music until 'prayer time,' when a few friends join us, when all who can, read the Scriptures, then a short address, and close with prayer.

After, comes the children's question time, then I try to stretch their intellect as soon as it offers to peep out, and to foster it where it does not exist.

My health is perfect; the climate agrees with me very well; sometimes I am in good spirits, and sometimes I am in the dumps, and think hard things of everything and everybody, myself included. You cannot understand my position till you have been two years and more tied to your post, eight days' journey from the nearest settlement; yet, if anyone would give me my choice today of any position, I could only say 'Wenzhou.' I would not change it, if I could, to rule a nation!"

After three and a half years' labour in the slums of Glasgow, my health being restored, I felt the time had come for me to go forth to China, and having in the meantime become engaged to Mr. Stott, I was sent out by the China Inland Mission to share his labours, to be as far as possible a helpmeet to him.

I sailed alone from London in the sailing ship, *Kai-sow,* on December 4, 1869, and prepared for the usual four months journey. A few days after, I laughingly said to the captain, "I want to get into Shanghai on the 12th of March."

He thought a moment and answered, "Not likely; if we do, it will be one of the fastest voyages on record. But," he asked, "why on the 12th of March?" I answered, "I had a fancy to get in on my birthday."

The captain was a kind and good man, and his influence was so felt over the ship that during that long voyage I never heard a word a lady might not hear from those sailors. He also encouraged me with meetings with the men, and as we had a pretty fair voyage, I was able to have one twice a week with them, nearly all the time. Two or three professed to receive blessing, but I do not know if they stood the test in later years. The captain and his dear wife became life-long friends.

In the Chinese seas we had a terrific storm, and as I had often longed to witness a real storm at sea, the captain jokingly said that he was sure I had prayed for this; the only consolation he had was that we could not now reach Shanghai on the 12th of March.

Nevertheless we anchored at Wusong on the eve of the 11th, and on the 12th, my twenty-fifth birthday, we arrived in Shanghai.

Mr. Stott met me there, and took me on to Ningbo, where I was kindly welcomed by Dr. Lord. According to Consular regulations then, I had to wait a month before we could be married, and on the 26th of April, 1870, we were made one in life, as we already were in heart. The day after our wedding, the cook Mr. Stott had brought with him from Wenzhou was baptized on profession of his faith.

It was my husband's desire to return at once to Wenzhou to his work, but nearly three weeks passed before he could find a ship to take us down. The coast was infested at that time with pirates, and ships were afraid to sail unless in fleets, under the protection of a warship. At last we sailed, and as we had a fair wind, expected to reach Wenzhou in three or four days; but alas! For our hopes, when we reached Zhoushan, only one tide from Ningbo river, the warship refused to proceed until other ships had joined the fleet; so there we had to stay for nine days, while the fairest of winds was blowing.

I was anxious to see my new home, and being fresh out from England and unaccustomed to the slow ways of the Chinese, my active temperament was sorely tried, as day after day we were put off with the promise we should leave by the next tide.

I bore the disappointment as well as I could, until the eighth day, when, woman-like, I had a good cry, which relieved my pent-up feelings. We were fifteen days between Ningbo and Wenzhou, a distance of only 150 miles.

Wenzhou itself is "beautiful for situation," having fertile mountains all round, and as we sailed slowly for days in and out amongst the islands, and then up the beautiful river, with grand mountains on either side, I almost fancied myself in dear old Scotland. Indeed the similarity has been remarked by many, except that instead of the clear blue lakes of the latter, we had the thick muddy water of the river. At that time Wenzhou was not an open port, and indeed it was not until seven years after this date that trading steamers were permitted to sail up her waters.

On reaching there we got a very hearty welcome from Mr. Jackson, who had come from Taizhou to take charge of Mr. Stott's work during his absence, but left soon after for his own station.

Never shall I forget the amount of excitement my presence caused; daily crowds of women came to see the first foreign lady who had been in their midst, and when I ventured out, it seemed as if the whole city was gathered to see me. At first I only went out in a sedan-chair, but the bearers were compelled to stand still while they looked at the strange object. Nor did they get easily over their curiosity. For a long time I was a strange thing to them, as if hardly human.

My first year in China was full of trial, being the ever memorable year of the "Tianjin Massacre." It was long after the event before we got details of that horrible crime. The natives seemed to know all about it before we did, and very soon the city was placarded with the vilest reports about us.

They said that at Tianjin all the foreigners had been killed or driven out of the place, because they kidnapped and murdered children, taking out their eyes, heart, and liver to compound into medicine. The same evil deeds were being done in this city. "Was it not known that we pretended to keep a school?" "Was it not true that so many children were missing?" "Had not some seen barrels in which were salted down babies?" "What was hard at Tianjin, was easy here, for there were but two; drive out the pests and let the city be at rest." Such were some of the expressions of the placards!

For about three months I hardly dared venture out of the house, and my husband was often met with stones and vile curses. For a few days there was a stream of people looking in every conceivable place for the said barrels; one of the school-boys was asked where the missing children were, and when he said it was all nonsense and lies, they said he had eaten the foreign medicine and would not tell. For a time my husband felt very anxious; if he had been alone he could have braved it, but the responsibility of another life seemed to weigh upon him.

One day he asked what I thought of a plan to leave for a few days on a ship, hoping when we returned all would be quiet. I saw it was on my account he made this suggestion, and when I answered that I feared if we left we might never get back again, and that I would rather stay and trust the Lord, he felt quite relieved.

Through the Lord's mercy we weathered that and many other storms; indeed, we got so used to threatening placards and having the day of our death posted up, which passed by as quietly as other days, that we began to feel less anxious about their threats. But in the midst of this time of suffering we were not without encouragement.

We got used to threatening placards and having the day of our death posted.

Mr. Stott wrote in September, 1870, to a dear friend:-

"Since I wrote you last, we have met with a few cheering circumstances. One came at a time when I was feeling cast down a little about the work. Owing to the massacre at Tianjin, we were in trouble and could not get out, and very few were coming in. One day a man came from the neighbouring prefecture, and said he wanted to see me. He told me he had been in company with a man who was a member here, and had heard him speak stories of Jesus Christ and of the God who created the heavens and the earth, and sent His Son to die for sinners; that they read the Bible every night together, and prayed to God to pardon and redeem them, and that he believed the 'doctrine' of Jesus and trusted on His merits for salvation, and that three or four others also believed. These I have never seen, but the man, who was a pedlar, and was in the city a few days refilling his pack, attended our evening worship every night, but has now gone again to pursue his business; also two of the boys are taking an interest in the truth; their minds are expanding and they most readily understand the Scriptures. Thus, often the Lord encourages us even in our darkest moments, though not always does the fruit, which seems so promising at the time, mature."

CHAPTER 3

They That Make Them

"They that make them are like unto them; so is every one that trusteth in them." Psalm 115:8

Another letter, dated March, 1871, describing idol worship and processions, gives some idea how excited the people get at such a time:-

"It is difficult to give information of idol worship, although I witnessed it daily, and idol processions are legion.

Idols in Wenzhou are usually made of a cross piece of wood to represent the body and arms, other pieces being fixed for legs. Then on the wood is twisted straw ropes to bring it as much as possible to the form required. On the straw is added clay, laid on in coats or layers, each having to dry before the next coat is added, the whole process taking some months if the idol is a large one.

The outer layer of clay is put on with much skill and care, as this must give expression to the countenance, etc. When dry, the painter smooths the cracks with putty, and paints in the orthodox fashion of its class. When all is finished there is generally a dedication feast, according to the rank of the idol; then it is established.

The idol is first worshipped at the feast of its dedication, and according to the merits it is said to possess. The worshipper brings two small candles and lights them on the altar with a few sticks of incense. After placing them on the altar, he kneels on the kneeboard (I have seen very many kneel, go through a course of bowing, and then turn round for their pipe, light it composedly at the burning candle, sit, and enjoy a smoke on the kneeboard); a few more prostrations, and the affair is over.

Processions are generally held in honour of some festival. There are shops where all the fixings are kept, and they usually contract for so many articles, according to the money they are able to raise, and only those streets get the procession through which can afford to contribute well. All the beauties in the neighbourhood wear their gala dresses, and come and sit in their doors, or at the street crossing, to see and be seen.

The procession is usually preceded by a band of boys gaudily dressed, bearing banners of gay and fantastic shapes, then a band of musicians, making the most unmusical, hideous sounds. A kind of pipe is conspicuous, but the universal gong is the most prominent, and pours forth a torrent of sound almost deafening.

Then comes the idol seated in an enormous sedan-chair carried by many bearers, the people kneeling and worshipping as it passes. I have seen the bearers streaming with perspiration under a vertical sun, and when it was set down wiping their tanned faces and falling on their knees before the disgusting object that was wasting their strength."

We lived at first in a small three-roomed Chinese house, having only the three upper rooms for ourselves - a bedroom, my husband's study, and the centre our living-room. The rooms below were the bedrooms of the schoolboys. We had then a fairly decent man for a cook, but utterly untaught; my husband had existed on any kind of food they could provide, and suffered much from indigestion as the result.

An amusing incident could be related to his experiences during this time; once being tired of rice three times a day, he asked his cook if he could not make him some cakes for breakfast.

He beamed encouragingly, and next morning there were hot cakes! But, oh! They were so solid and hard and with a lump of fat pork in the centre.

Not relishing this, and yet not willing to discourage budding genius, he waited till all had gone to bed that night, and abstracted from the tiny larder all the pork that could be found.

The next morning the hot cakes came as before. What could be in the centre this time? There was no pork in the house, so he was curious. Very suspiciously, the white mass was not pork, but was found to be nothing more hurtful than a piece of turnip.

After that cakes were given up.

Instead of sitting down quietly and learning the language, as I would have liked, I had to put my house in order, which was not to be done in a day.

The cook had to be taught how to cook, and the coolie had to be taught how to wash and iron clothes, clean, scrub, etc. Thanks to the early training of a careful grandmother, these things were not much of a trouble to me, except in the matter of bread-making.

Time after time I tried to produce bread without yeast, following the recipes of cookery books, with the result that the bread might have done for hearthstones, but not for food. My husband encouraged me by saying it had a good taste, though it was a little hard; but for his patience I would probably have given up long before success crowned my efforts.

Some of my experiences in those early days were both trying and amusing.

I remember one day, after having spent the morning teaching the coolie how to wash clothes, I had put a boilerful on to boil, and telling him not to touch them till I came back, I retired for an hour's rest. On returning I lifted the lid of the boiler, when to my horror I saw dark blue water and my clothes dyed dark; the coolie thought it a good opportunity of putting in his blue calico shirt, which was more lively than comfortable.

Of course my work had to be done all over again.

I found not only the school-children's clothing but my husband's claimed my attention. He had been put to some queer straits in his efforts to keep his stockings mended. Of course no Chinese knew how to mend such things, and he had nearly as little idea himself.

One day, while looking in his box for something to fill up a large hole, he spied a dress-coat which he had brought from England with him. It was useless as it was, so he thought it would do for mending; cutting off one of the tails and spreading it on the floor, he put his foot on the top, made a chalk mark all round, leaving a good flap to turn over.

It was a good evening's work, and when I ruthlessly cut off the feet of the said stockings he boasted they had lasted two years. The coat afterwards was given to his teacher, and, though minus a tail, kept him warm for several years under his Chinese garment.

Flannels, too, were in a sad condition. Of course they did not know how to wash such things. When I asked how they came to be this peculiar colour (a greenish yellow), he explained that the first time they were washed the coolie had put them into a tub, and poured the thick muddy water of the river over them, thus leaving them for a day or two; when washed and returned to Mr. Stott the hardness suggested a shaking, when the clouds of dust almost blinded him.

With so many other duties it was not to be expected that I could learn the language very fast. I was distressed after nearly two years to find, though able to·speak enough for household matters, I was unable to teach the Gospel to the women who almost daily visited me.

My husband had engaged a Christian woman at Ningbo to help me in caring for the schoolboys. She loved to go with her hymnbook and New Testament visiting among the women. I was too ignorant at the time to know how little her Ningbo dialect was understood by our Wenzhou women. Perhaps it was well I did not know, for it comforted me greatly to do her work, while I sent her out daily to teach the women about the Saviour's love.

My health, too, suffered much from the climate. The second year I had a very severe illness, which nearly cost me my life.

One day, while in a very low condition, my husband was called away to save a man who had eaten opium; he was loth to leave me, too weak to make my wants known to others, but I urged him to go, for I was sorely tried by the thought that I was hindering instead of helping him, as I so longed to do.

He had been gone, perhaps, about an hour. It was a hot day in July, and I suppose partly from the heat and partly from my weakness I fainted; when I recovered consciousness my bed was surrounded on all sides by school-boys, teachers, and servants who had come to wail, thinking I was dead.

One had run off for Mr. Stott, and meeting him on the way back, cried: "Oh, master, come back; mistress is dead!" Hoping it might be only a faint, he hurried home and found me restored to consciousness.

I remember so well, when able to sit up a little, how I longed for two things, either of which I thought would make me well - the sight of one of my country women, or a little beef-tea, neither of which were within my reach.

In those days we were not well off in the matter of food. We had but little communication with the outside world except by letter. Once in two years we took a holiday, when we brought in necessary stores to last us the next two years, for in the city of Wenzhou we could neither get beef or mutton, milk, potatoes, or butter.

But these were by no means our greatest hardships. The indifference of the people affected us more than our surroundings.

But these were by no means our greatest hardships. The indifference of the people affected us more than our surroundings.

After the second year I had the servants trained, so that I could give most of my time to missionary work. I began first by visiting their homes, and everywhere I was well received, being a curiosity to be looked and wondered at. They thought it strange I should speak their language, but they had little heart for my message. Alas! They did not know they needed a Saviour. About this time my husband and Mr. Jackson, who had joined us about the end of my first year, rented a large shop in the busy part of the city for a chapel. They fitted up one part of it as a bookshop, and a native preacher sat daily selling books and preaching to all who might come in, and in the afternoon the large chapel was thrown open, when either my husband or Mr. Jackson preached.

At first crowds came to hear, but after a time they dropped off, and the ones and the twos who really wanted to be taught came to listen.

An extract from Mr. Stott's letter describes the kind of crowd he often had to deal with:

"When the gates are opened, in rushes every one near-street strollers and loungers, rowdies, travelling tradesmen of all kinds, hawkers crying out their wares, conjurors, fortune-tellers, musicians, thieves and beggars; the shaven pate of a Buddhist priest, the cowl of the Touist priest may also be seen, and the noise is almost beyond description.

I assure you it is no easy task to arrest or keep the attention of such a crowd, and it is a great strain upon the lungs and intellect, as I have proved yesterday by experience. In the forenoon I kept nearly every eye fixed, every mouth open, and every tongue quiet for more than three-quarters of an hour, while I told them of the origin of sin, its effects, and salvation through our Redeemer. Many listened attentively all the time; the greater portion flit about, go and come, and never sit down. My daily prayer is that our chapel may be the birthplace of many souls. Yesterday far more than a thousand people heard; it takes long for them to understand, but by God's blessing we are giving 'line upon line ' as they are able to receive it."

About the same time he refers to the conversion of the two eldest boys in the school; they, with two other boys, were baptized soon after. A letter written by these boys to the same friend, who had shown them much kindness, is here inserted, and may be interesting as a specimen of Chinese composition.

Honoured and respected Sir,

We, the undermentioned boys, in the tenth moon and twenty-seventh day received a letter from you, which our teacher, Mr. Stott, translated for us. You have for a long time shown us much kindness, and your kind exhortations to us are very good.

We Wenzhou boys, although the road is very long, seem so near as almost to eat with you at the same table. We cannot thank you enough for the interest you take in us.

In the first place, we want to thank you for the beautiful pictures you sent us, although in themselves not of infinite value, yet they manifest a loving heart. Also you continually pray for us ignorant boys, that in school we may increase knowledge and continue in good bodily condition; also that in reading the Bible we may understand and know about God. We also do a little at the books of the native sages, and are able to understand somewhat, because you pray for us, but your very humble servants know but little of propriety; we also forget your grace, and have no grace to give you in return; our faces are like brass, and our necks stiff as iron-forgive us.

By the grace of God in the former part of this year a chapel was opened in the Five Horse Street, and very many have heard the gospel. At first they were very noisy and understood but little, now there is a great difference for the better; they are willing to sit quietly and listen. To preach is also far less difficult. Also, before we removed, our sleeping rooms were much hampered; but we are better here - the rooms are large and can accommodate five or six easily: no matter how many come, there is room.

"At worship we every morning and evening read the Scriptures and pray to God. At present in the mornings we are reading the Book of Jeremiah the prophet of God, how the Lord sent him to the King of Judah with a message; but the king would not listen to him, but hardened his heart, and disgraced the prophet by putting him into a dungeon; but the Lord vindicated His servant, and manifested His power by punishing that king and his people.

At evening worship we are reading the fifth book of the New Testament, the Acts of the Apostles; we are at the ninth chapter, where Saul persecuted the disciples of Jesus. He was fierce as a lion, and intended to eat up the disciples, by means of a letter from the authorities at Jerusalem; but on the way to Damascus he met the Lord, who changed his heart, and from that day till the day of his death he served the Lord. The mystery of God we are unable to understand, but we are sincere in our worship. We pray that the grace of God may be abundantly to you, and yours, to all generations.

P.S. - When you see errors in our writing or our composition, pass lightly over, and don't laugh at us, for we are already ashamed of ourselves.

Written at the school-house of Wenzhou, tenth moon, twenty-seventh day.

SENG SI NYU,

TSIU DIE CHENG,

Wenchow School-boys, School Teacher, Mrs. Stott, and Miss Bardsley. The front row were converted and three of the six are now unpaid preachers.

"For all the rest."

Mr. Stott writes,

There are many things to give trouble and anxiety; it is not all smooth sailing, nor yet all success. If we were to sum up our defeats, I am sure it would be easy for me to show ten failures for one success.

In writing of the difficulties of sustained teaching, he adds

When the novelty of reading or speaking God's Word wears off, it needs a strong hold within the veil to sustain us; only close living and walking with God can do this, and my experience leads me to the conclusion that it can only be got or maintained by living, active faith and prayer - real prayer, the soul grappling like Jacob, getting strength, not weakness, from the struggle.

In November, 1871, we had an interesting case of conversion - that of a Buddhist priest.

After he had believed the truth he left his monastery, returned to his native village, and began farm work. He was most earnest in telling all whom he met of the God who had saved him, and we had hoped for fresh openings through his efforts; but only a few months after his baptism, while on his way to join us in a communion service, his boat was overturned in a storm, and our brother, with twenty-eight others, found a watery grave.

It is to this man Mr. Stott refers in the following,

Last night three elderly men from the country remained to inquire further about the 'doctrine,' and seemed in earnest. Our friend, the Bhuddist priest, has come, and begs not to be sent away again without baptism. He says that in and round his village twenty-eight people believe the Gospel, and have turned from idolatry.

That statement must be modified, and perhaps really means that about that number acquiesce in what he says about worshipping idols, and of the only living and true God; but allowing it to be modified, there is still a good margin in his favour. If he has faithfully told twenty-eight persons all he knows, that is something.

He says he is known for ten miles round as the turncoat priest."

Two years later there was another interesting case of a man who had been a priest all his life, and was over seventy when he first heard the Gospel; he attended more or less regularly for two or three years, and then asked to be baptized; but was told he could not be a follower of Christ while wearing the priestly garb, and living on the gains of idolatry. This was a sore disappointment; he was an old man, unable to work, and had no other means of livelihood.

This was a case we longed to help, but feared the result upon the young church. He continued in the temple, but got others to perform his priestly duties. He was troubled at not being baptized, so one day, putting on clean garments, he went to a mountain stream nearby, prayed on the bank, then plunged in and baptized himself!

A few days afterwards he met with one of the Christians, and asked whether he thought that baptism would do; but the Christian was unable to give him any information, never having heard of such a case before. It was not long ‘ere we heard of the fruit of this man's labour.

Mr. Stott, writing to a friend a few months afterwards, says:

During the last ten days three new inquirers have come; one, an old man near seventy, has been a vegetarian for nearly forty years, and has been to all the temples in the district worshipping.

Lately, he went to a temple some distance from his home to burn candles. While worshipping, the priest saw him, and after making sure there was no one to hear, said, 'Elder brother, I have been a priest for sixty years, and worshipped these things until two years ago; but they never did me any good, and never will. You, like myself, are an old man, and must soon die. Come inside and I will tell you who, and how, to worship.'

He then took him into his room and preached Jesus to him. The question naturally arose, 'Where did you hear such things?'

'From the foreigners in the city.'

'From the foreigners!' he exclaimed; 'why, there is no crime under heaven but the foreigners have committed, and they are going to be beheaded one of these days, if indeed it be not already done.'

The priest assured him that was untrue, and told him he had been to Wenzhou only three days before, and had listened to the true words of God. The priest informed him that some tens of good men had entered the religion, and were going to eternal happiness in heaven; he, too, would have joined them, but he was too old to earn his rice, and had nothing to depend on but the temple, and the missionary had said he could not be a disciple of Jesus and eat the rice of idols.

All this and much more the poor old priest told him; also of pardon and peace through Jesus, God's Son. He died in the temple, but, we believe, a true disciple.

About this time a man from Shenyang dropped in to hear the foreigner.

He was interested, and had a long talk with the native preacher. He had a good many questions to ask, and returned home to think. He came again and again, and, after a while, truly received the truth. He had been told that opium growing was nearly as bad as opium smoking. He had some growing in his fields, and his conscience became troubled.

One night he was trying to argue with himself. He was poor and it paid better than anything else. It was too late in the season to grow wheat. He would let it alone this year, but give it up the following.

He could not sleep, however. The question troubled him more than he liked. At last he rose by dawn, took his scythe, and cut down every root of opium. He was baptized soon after, and, when we visited him two years later, we found his wife and mother true Christians.

He also conducted morning and evening prayers, when eleven of his neighbours joined him.

Surely this was an instance of what a sincere heart and simple eye to God can do. He had but little ability, but what he had he used for God.

CHAPTER 4

A Mischievous Device

"They imagined a mischievous device, which they are not able to perform," Psalm 21:11

In April, 1873, Mr. Stott paid his first visit into the Dong-ling district, and thus writes,

Last week I made a journey into the country, to a place distant about twenty miles from here.

Two days before I went to a village about six miles off, and when I returned I found my pony's back sadly hurt by the saddle. There was nothing for it but to rest him for two days and re-stuff my saddle, which was a difficult job for me.

At the time appointed, accompanied by one of the members, and a man to carry my bed, I got off pretty early. It was a lovely spring morning, and the road we had to travel was beautiful in the extreme. I heard the frogs croaking for the first time this season; the oil plant was in full bloom, filling the air with fragrance; farmers were sowing~ the early rice, and the bamboo groves were full of the melody of singing birds. The snakes also were out sunning themselves and wriggling their ugly forms on the sides of the path.

After riding about five miles or so, we struck the foot of the hills, and after dinner we came to the district we had in view, and I rode from hamlet to hamlet, preaching and selling books. The whole district soon turned out to see and hear, for there had never been a foreigner in that place before. We could see men in the fields a mile off throw down their hoes and run as if for life, and all to see your humble servant. As we advanced the crowds gathered more thick and noisy.

One cannot judge of the noise of a Chinese crowd till they have heard one; nobody listens, but everybody shouts at the top of his voice, and such shrill, piercing sounds, no Saxon throat could produce anything like them.

I continued preaching until nearly sundown, then went to the house where we were to pass the night; but the scene there would need a livelier pen than mine to give even an outline of it.

At last, almost in despair, I took my crutch and gave a knock on the wooden partition, and ordered every tongue to be still and listen to me. To my surprise I succeeded in getting them quieted pretty well, and then preached salvation through Jesus Christ till my throat was sore.

Then the man who carried my bed took up the subject and showed them that idols made of wood and clay could not do any one good, and exhorted them all to worship the only living and true God, who had sent Jesus Christ, His dear Son, to open the way of heaven for them, and who is now there interceding for those who trust Him.

Most of the people left to get their evening rice, but soon returned in greater force than ever; and, though tired and weary, I had to begin again and preach to a late hour.

Then I asked all to leave and return in the morning, but just as I was going to bed a deputation from the elders of the village came, saying that all the wisest of the old men were in a house near by and wanted a quiet interview, to hear and see for themselves, for the youngsters had brought strange news.

This was a rare good chance of speaking for our blessed Saviour, and lifting up my heart to Him for guidance, He gave it, and enabled me to speak of His Holy Name.

I continued for nearly an hour to address fourteen men, who listened most attentively all the time. One asked 'how to worship this true God.'

I told him, and knelt on the wet mud floor and prayed for them all, thanked God for His goodness in giving them life and food, and asked Him to send the Holy Spirit to teach them and open their hearts.

When I got up they all were surprised; some looking at me with amazement, not knowing what to make of it. One asked, 'But will God hear you?'

I answered, 'Your own books tell you that heaven has eyes, which is true; would it not be strange if heaven had eyes and no ears?' They all replied, 'True, true.'"

At a very late hour they left, and I could not help thanking God for such a golden opportunity of setting His Name before so many people.

These preaching tours were continued as often as possible. Sometimes I would accompany him to the nearer places, but more often I had to remain to look after home affairs.

Referring to another of these tours, Mr. Stott writes,

Some three weeks ago I had an interesting preaching tour.

We visited a good many towns and villages, and had often over a thousand listeners; sometimes we preached from the theatre stand, or in the village temple, or again, when no good situation was obtainable, from my horse's back.

I had two Christian natives with me, who also preached in turn. One, however lost his voice after the second day, but the other continued to speak. He could be heard a quarter of a mile off.

I have seldom listened to a voice equal to his. Perhaps the late lamented Duncan Matheson's was as good, but Duncan's was a deep bass, and the native I refer to was a shrill tenor, and anything but pleasing. However; he preached Jesus Christ plainly and fully. These stayed about ten days after I left, and preached in a few other places."

I did not feel comfortable in staying away too long, with Mrs. Stott all alone, and so many people to look after; but she can get along much better now, can speak pretty well, and is making good progress in the Chinese character.

She goes out to visit twice a week, and has a daily class of the smaller boys, and an advanced Bible-class on Sunday afternoons. Besides she takes the entire charge of the food and clothing of the school; that with the addition of our own affairs and her Chinese studies, keeps her busy, such that she seldom has an hour to spare; but I am thankful to say she is in good health.

I wish I had time to refer in greater detail to the many places visited at this time. One, in particular, struck me as being the most lovely I have ever seen; but the people seemed sadly degraded. The village was situated in a glen of almost horse-shoe shape; at the back and sides the hills rose high and abrupt, assuming almost the aspect of mountains, while on in front was a long plain, widening as it went. A beautiful stream ran past the village, which we crossed; the gardens seemed full of fruit, oranges, pomeloes, and pomegranates, all ripening on the trees.

The head family of the village took us in for the night and treated us well. After supper the people came crowding in, and I preached to them to a late hour, while the natives who were with me had a still larger audience in the reception hall. They treated me thus kindly because I had formerly cured one of the ladies when ill with fever."

Next morning I was up, had breakfast, and in the saddle again at sunrise, and made our way to another village, when the whole population turned out to the temple yard. I climbed on to the theatre stand and preached in turn with the native assistant. By and by the head priest raised some objection to our preaching in front of the gods.

I said if the people objected I would go somewhere else; but most cried, 'No, no, stop where you are.' One of the crowd called out, 'If the priest is not quiet, we will carry him to the top of the hill and make him fast to a tree.'

That remark caused a good deal of merriment at the expense of the poor priest, who remained quiet for the rest of the time. As I wanted to push on I did not accept the kind hospitality of the village schoolmaster, who wished to detain me to dinner."

After this, quite a number in Dong-ling became interested, and my husband was invited to go and preach to them. He did so, with the result that a little church was formed in the house of one of the members.

One day Mr. Stott had gone to Dong-ling in the hope of finding a house he could rent as a chapel.

On the day I expected him home a man came from there bringing me a large fish as a present, and saying Mr. Stott had found a place for a chapel, and had sent him for money to settle the matter. The present of the fish was a little suspicious.

I asked whether he had not a letter for me, and he said he had, but on stepping out of the boat it had dropped into the canal and was lost. A few more questions revealed the rogue, and as I spoke of sending for Yamen runners, he ran off, leaving the fish behind him. A little later my husband returned, and as we discussed the fish at tea we laughed over the clumsy attempt at fraud.

I think it was in 1873 or 1874 we were surprised one morning by a strange man coming in with a small bundle of bedding on his back. Almost his first words were, "I have come to stay and be taught the doctrine."

We did not receive people in that easy fashion, but when my husband sat down to talk with him he heard a strange story.

The man had been a soldier during the Taiping rebellion. He left father, mother, and a young wife to serve his country, and was absent two or three years. During his absence his wife had died, though his father and mother were still alive. He had become disgusted with what he had seen of the world, and had determined to give himself up to a religious life.

What money he had he spent in purchasing coffins for his father and mother, and making their graves! Having fulfilled this filial duty he retired to the hills to lead a holy life. He built himself a very small hut, with bed and bedding too short to lie down in, compelling himself to rest in a sitting posture. He soon got a name for sanctity, and the people of the neighbouring villages brought him presents of food in return for his prayers.

One day a man was passing the house of a Christian, and on being asked by him where he was going, replied, "To the hermit with a present."

"Oh," said the Christian; "wait a moment, I, too, have a present for him." He brought out a Gospel, and asking the young man to give it to the holy man on the hill, went on with his work, probably thinking no more of the matter.

Some days after this the hermit saw the young man again, and asked where that book came from.

He answered, "I suppose from the foreigner in Wenzhou, but I know little about it. My neighbour talks about a true God, and one Jesus Christ; but I don't understand."

The poor hermit became restless to know something more about this strange doctrine, and for the first time in three years he came down the hill and walked to Wenzhou to inquire after the true God. After hearing his story, my husband invited him to stay with us for a week, and seeing his diligent study of the Bible and eagerness to learn, asked him to stay on a few weeks longer.

One morning, while I was having a Bible-class with the schoolboys and others who had joined, the subject being John 3, I saw this man weeping. My husband took him aside and asked him what was the matter.

He only answered, "My sins, my sins!"

It was the first time we had seen a Chinaman weep because of sin, and it thrilled us through and through. He never returned to the hill again, but in his home he found too much opposition to contend with, and, strange to say, though we sent time after time, and prayed much for him, he never entered into the truth. After a year or so he led us to understand he did not care for us to send to him any more, as his parents did not want him to become a Christian.

But the young man who had carried the book to him, and of whom we had never thought, began to wonder what was in that book, to cause the man to come down from the hill and break his vow of sanctity. He inquired further into the truth and after a time, was converted, and through him his father, mother, and aunt became Christians, and are still in the church.

We had often trials and disappointments through the duplicity and love of gain, which is so common in the Chinese character; a man would profess a most earnest desire for the truth, and seem to hold it very precious, while all the time his hope was that he would get employment of some kind.

A case in point was a school teacher, who seemed to be converted, and almost daily would, of his own accord, stop the boys in their studies to read the Bible and pray with them. He had been an opium smoker, but professed to have given it up when he became a Christian; but later on he went back to his opium and gave up all profession of faith in Christ. He had two boys in school, who, after the usual term of education, were apprenticed to trades; for a long while we lost sight of them, but a few years ago the eldest of them was truly converted, and is now one of our volunteer unpaid preachers.

There was another who deceived us for years. He had been a fortune-teller, but when he professed to receive the Gospel he gave up everything of the kind, and seemed to be very earnest in telling his friends and neighbours the Good News. This brought some persecution upon him, which he bore bravely. At last they trumped up a case against him. He was taken to the Yamen and accused of crimes he had never committed. The mandarin told him plainly that if he would renounce this foreign religion he might be set free; but he answered, "You may cut my head off, but I will never renounce the Christian religion!"

The mandarin told him plainly that if he would renounce this foreign religion he might be set free, but he answered, "You may cut my head off, but I will never renounce the Christian religion!"

He was kept in prison for nearly three months, and we were powerless to help him.

We were much touched by his steadfastness, and began to think that after all we must be wrong in our want of confidence in him, for somehow we never could quite trust him.

He farmed his own land, but spent much of his time in volunteer preaching, so that through his efforts the work began to grow much in the Dong-ling district. The question of employing him often came up in our minds, for we were sorely in need of teachers in those early days, but this feeling we had, of not being quite sure of our man, kept my husband from doing so.

He grew tired of waiting, and, after a little agitation, boldly went over to the Roman Catholics, saying that he had waited for seven years in the hope of employment, and that if we would not pay him he would have nothing to do with us.

The Roman Catholics employed him, and the true character came out in his determined efforts to upset our work. He had brought many of these men into the church, and meant to take them out if he could, but happily he had been the means of bringing in better men than himself, and only a very few halting ones followed him; but he was a thorn in our flesh for many years.

About the year 1874, we passed through a series of difficulties through evil reports. If there was evil in the city the foreigner must be at the bottom of it.

A secret society, called the "ring" society, had sprung up.

Mr. Stott was said to be the head and moving spirit. All who chose to join would receive a gold ring and four dollars, but they would be pledged to do all in their power to upset the present government.

Mr. Stott was pestered for gold rings and dollars, and one day, making sure that an applicant knew what he was doing, and was ready for any villainy, he felt the time had come to put a stop to it.

Sending his card to the Yamen, he asked them to take charge of the man and to inquire into the case. Two Yamen runners were at once sent, and before they had taken him outside the gate they had possessed themselves of his best garments and hat. After a few days my husband requested the man might be set at liberty, and we were no more troubled with the "ring" society.

An uneasy feeling was all over the city at this time. A band had been organised amongst the hills for a raid upon the city. They were known to be strong, and of course the foreigner was said to be at the head. It had been working for months. The authorities took alarm, and sent to Taizhou for troops. Cannons were placed upon the city walls, the gates closed each night at sunset, and a mandarin placed upon guard until daybreak.

We knew our name was connected with this uprising, but we had passed through so many storms of the kind that my husband and Mr. Jackson left me, as usual, to visit the out-stations, and expected to be away nearly a fortnight.

They had only been gone a few days, when the school teacher came to me in great alarm, and said the city was posted with violent placards. Mr. Stott, they said, had gone to train and organise the band, while I was taking in large quantities of rice in order to feed them when they came.

The teacher said there was great danger of an attack upon us, and urged me to write to the mandarin and request protection. I thought and prayed over the matter, and finally decided to wait patiently for the return of my husband.

In answer to prayer they came home four or five days earlier than expected. Mr. Stott at once wrote the authorities denying these statements, stating we were quiet and peaceable people, bent only on preaching peace to all men, and that we had nothing to do with any kind of society, and asking for a proclamation to this effect. This the mandarin granted, but his proclamations were no sooner up than they were torn down, or bespattered with mud. The people seemed bent on mischief, and we were warned by friendly neighbours we had better leave. But how could we leave the few sheep we had gathered in from the wilderness? They did not know the heart of the Shepherd.

At last things got so threatening that our servants were warned to leave us. An attack, they said, had been decided upon for the following Tuesday, and if they did not go they would probably share our fate.

So, on the Saturday our two servants, and the woman who looked after the boys, said they must leave us that day.

My husband called me downstairs to tell me the sorrowful news. It was evident the servants were frightened, and I thought we should be better without timid people about us. Our coolie had recently professed conversion, and it was a bitter disappointment that he should leave us in our hour of need.

We had expected the hatred of the heathen, but not the desertion of the Christian. Without expressing any regret we offered him his wages with the others, but he refused to take them, saying he would be back in a week. "Yes, after we are killed, or the danger over," were the words that arose in my heart. But I was soon to be ashamed of such unkind thoughts, for in about an hour he returned and begged to be allowed to stay. The others returned a week later, when they saw we were still alive.

We had expected the hatred of the heathen, but not the desertion of the Christian.

This coolie had rather a hasty temper, which sometimes brought him into trouble. One evening, while we were at prayer, we could hardly hear our own voices for the noise of quarrelling downstairs. Mr. Stott went to see what was the matter, and found the coolie and one of the elder boys had quarrelled. He spoke seriously to them, remarking that it was very sad, after all the teaching, that we should be disturbed while in prayer by their quarrels.

The coolie hastily produced the horsewhip; putting it in front of Mr. Stott, and himself in position for whipping, he remarked, "I am the one most to blame, whip me." He was told he must go to God to seek and find forgiveness; and this, I have no doubt, he did, but he seemed disappointed that he was not whipped also.

Of course I had all the housework to do in the meantime.

We were not, however, without real anxiety, for there was no doubt that an attack upon the city was intended, and we knew if the robbers came we should suffer both at their hands and at the hands of the enraged people, who looked upon us as the cause of all their suffering. So we made a few private plans.

A long rope was secured and kept in a convenient place. This was to let us over the city wall, where we could fly towards the sea. But we hardly knew what to do with a few of our school boys who had no homes. A friendly neighbour promised that he would give us the first alarm, so that we might have time to escape.

One midnight a terrific knocking at the gate aroused us from our first sleep. In a moment we were on the verandah listening breathlessly to know what it could be. The man who had promised to tell us of the first danger rushed in crying, "Mr. Stott, get away as soon as you can; the insurgents have broken in the west gate, trampled upon the mandarin, and are now making their way through the city."

My husband went down to gather our people together to see who would go with us to share our uncertain fate, but first he dispatched a messenger to find out if the news was really true.

Downstairs they were having prayer, commending us all to God, while I was upstairs preparing for flight. It was warm weather, so I only had to roll a flannel coat for my husband and a thin gown for myself, which made a very small parcel, tying twenty dollars round my waist, and putting the rest into a bag tied to the neck of a bottle in which were secured the title-deeds of the house, intending to sink them into the well.

These few preparations being completed I went downstairs, rope in one hand and small bundle in the other. Even to this sad picture there was a ludicrous side, for we were gravely asked by one of the elder boys "what were we going to do with the furniture?"

The messenger returned saying the news was true, and we had better get off as soon as possible; but I knew from the short time I had been upstairs it was impossible for him to have been to the west gate and back. I suggested to Mr. Stott to ask him, and he acknowledged that he had not, but all the city was talking about it.

He was again despatched, with orders to run all the way, and, if true, to run back with all haste, and we might still have time to escape. Oh, what a long, long time it seemed! Every moment was precious, and might mean life to us.

At last he returned, only to say it was a false alarm. A band of thieves had spread the report, and when the poor people, panic-stricken, ran from their houses, they went in and helped themselves. We thanked God, went to bed, and slept soundly till morning.

During those early years it seemed impossible to live without offence before the people.

For instance, my husband built a chimney, and though not very high, immediately it was conjectured to be a signalling apparatus to communicate with steamers; a neighbour's child took ill and died, and the unfortunate chimney was found to be the cause.

A deputation waited upon us to request that the chimney should be pulled down. This was done, but soon afterwards someone else in the neighbourhood took ill, and the cause this time was found to be my husband's stable - that, too, must come down.

My husband explained that he could not afford the expense, but as it was for their own benefit they were at liberty to pull down the obnoxious thing and rebuild any shape they approved at their own expense. This settled the question, and the poor horse's stable was left untouched.

Another time, while Mr. Stott was preaching in the chapel to a large and seemingly attentive audience, he happened to look at his watch, when a man asked, "What is that he is looking at?" The reply was, "A kind of hocus-pocus instrument whereby he can tell how many are to be hocussed by his preaching, and when they are hocussed to the desired number and extent he will stop."

Mr. Stott knew nothing of this till some time afterwards when, going into the country, he found the whole place full of the absurd story.

CHAPTER 5

Our Lord Is Above All Gods

Our Lord is above all gods." Psalm 135:5

It was about this time my husband sent a preacher to open up work in the city of Bing-yie.

As usual, crowds came to listen at first, but soon dropped off, and he, feeling rather lonely, asked that someone might be sent to help him. We had no one to send, so my husband sent a Christian schoolboy, named Z-nüe, thirteen years of age, for a few months to keep him company.

One day the lad entered into a heathen temple; he could not see worshippers, but at every shrine there were lighted candles and incense, showing some one had been there. Turning round, he saw an old man just finishing his obeisance to the last of the numerous gods, and as he sat down to rest the lad addressed him.

"Venerable grand-father," said he, "why do you worship these idols? They are made of clay, and can neither see, hear, or help you. Indeed they cannot help themselves, for see, some of their fingers are broken off, and others have had the hair of their moustachios stolen by rats. Rats do not steal the hair of your moustache: why? Because you are a living man. How foolish, then, to worship these things which even the rats may rob with impunity. Not only so; do not the rats make their nests inside these very idols?"

The old man sighed, and said, "What am I to do?"

The lad then told him of the God in heaven, and of Jesus Christ His Son, and the way of salvation that had been provided for "whosoever will."

The old man listened with great astonishment, he had never heard such wisdom. As he was deeply interested, he was invited to the chapel to hear more from the preacher. He not only came himself, but brought his old wife; and after a time they both became truly converted, and for years led godly, consistent lives.

The aged couple are now in glory.

This young lad, who was converted when he was about twelve, afterwards became an earnest and successful preacher in this very city of Bing-yie. I remember Mr. Stott, in speaking, before sending him out on his first mission, told him he was to preach Christ, and to leave idolatry and their idols and idol customs alone; for as soon as truth entered into their heart the other would soon go out.

After talking for some time he asked the boy if he understood what he meant.

He said, "Yes, you mean like this: the people are now living in an old tumbled-down hut, and you don't want me to pull this down about their ears. I am, as it were, to build a beautiful house, furnished with all good things, and then invite them to leave their old broken-down hut and enter into their new possession."

That young man laboured earnestly, preaching often in the open air; by and by consumption manifested itself, and in spite of all our efforts, so precious, and as it seemed to us so necessary, a life in the early stage of our work, ended.

He died, twenty-five years of age. That was a great loss to the young church, for he had been well taught and trained by Mr. Stott.

In 1872, our cook, who was baptized the day after our marriage, married a heathen girl. We were grieved, yet what could we do? To insist that the Christians should marry only in the Lord was practically to forbid marriage, seeing there were no Christian women within seven days' journey of them.

The influence of the heathen wife was soon apparent, first in coldness of heart, then in utter indifference to spiritual things, and before two years were over we had to dismiss him from the church. This led us to see that something must be done to supply the great need of Christian wives for our Christian young men, if we would have a strong and healthy church.

So, after much prayer and thought on the subject we decided to commence a girls' boarding-school. There were many difficulties in the way. We had no suitable accommodation for girls. Then we determined we would have no bound feet, and that we knew would probably prevent our getting the kind of girls we wanted.

Some other schools had felt it necessary to continue this evil practice, because of this very difficulty; and one school that I knew of had found it very hard to contend against this almost universal custom. But we felt the importance of being pioneers, and were anxious to begin on a solid basis, that others could build upon.

It was better we should fight these questions at first, rather than start on easier lines and have the battle to face later on. We therefore gave out that we were prepared to take in a few girls under ten years of age, that we should feed, clothe and educate them free of expense to their parents, but we should require that their feet be unbound, and that we should have the right to betroth them to those whom we thought fit persons, and that the parents should have no power to betroth them without our consent.

At this time we only had one old woman in the church, and she was the first to bring me her grand-daughter. I explained clearly that her feet would be unbound. To this and the other rules she cheerfully consented.

The child was a dear little thing, nine years of age, and being the only one, I had her with me a good deal and of course became very fond of her.

When the parents saw this, they thought the time had come to make a fuss about her feet. They seemed to think I should be sure to give way rather than lose the pretty little thing that was so winning; so one day a message was brought to me that the child's mother had been crying night and day, for some time; that she was then tearing her hair, bemoaning the fate of her child who should grow up with feet like a man; she would never get a husband, for who would care for a girl with large feet? She therefore requested me to send her home, as she would rather beg from door to door than see her daughter so disgraced.

I told the messenger they had brought her of their own free will; they understood our terms, and had agreed to them; that if they wanted her back they must come and fetch her, but first they must pay me the expenses of food and clothing, the amount which I had expended upon her. Of course they were unable to do this, and as I was firm they unwillingly gave in, and so our first battle against foot-binding was fought and won.

Still there was a great difficulty in getting girls, owing to this question, and for several years we had to be content with four, two of whom we certainly would not have received later on when our position was established and the benefits of the school manifested.

The girls' school has now been in existence twenty-two years, and has proved a great blessing to the church.

The girls have had a thoroughly practical training, and most of them become Christian workers after they leave school.

During the last ten years, twenty-two girls have been married, three only of whom have left school unconverted. There are seven or eight of our married girls who take regular classes among women and children. For nearly ten years we saw but little spiritual fruit, two or three professed to believe on Jesus, but there was no corresponding power or change in their lives.

Our Bible-readings seemed the most wearisome part of the day to them, and they appeared to have no spiritual perception. For the first few years, while the children were young, I did not feel the burden, perhaps, as heavily as I ought to have done; but as years passed on I became almost desperate. Many a time I have gone from the school to my room with literal tears, sobbing, "Will these girls never be saved?" But, in 1884, the Lord was pleased to visit us with a very gracious revival.

There was no indication of the coming blessing, save that the elder girls were more attentive than usual with the Bible lessons.

Wenchow School-girls and Teachers. Left, Miss Whitford ; right, Miss Chalmers.

One morning in June we were sitting as usual at our work, the elder girls a little apart with their needlework, while I was surrounded by a group of little ones whom I was teaching to sew and knit. The quiet was suddenly disturbed by the eldest girl saying: "Teacher, do you think if I came to Christ now, He would save me?"

I looked at the girl, there was an expression of earnestness on her face I never had seen before. She continued, "You have often urged me to come to Christ, but I have never been willing; will He take me now?"

I could hardly speak for the joy that welled up in my heart. I answered, “Oh, yes,” and began to tell her of my own conversion when I was two years younger than she. While I spoke, she burst into tears, and with a cry and sob ran from the room. I could contain myself no longer, but with tears of joy I ran into my husband's study and cried: “Blessing is coming at last; Ah-Mai is seeking the Lord.

We knelt together to pour out our thanksgiving, after which I returned to the girls. I found Ah-Mai in her room. We knelt together by her bed while I asked God to have mercy upon her soul, to save her then and there; and thinking it best to leave her alone for a time, I returned to the schoolroom.

Two other girls were sobbing, and when I asked what was the matter they answered, “We are such sinners.”

I called them upstairs, that I might quietly point them to the Saviour, but their distress was so great they could hardly listen.

One sobbed, “You don't know how bad I have been," and going to her cupboard she took out pieces of calico and little odds and ends I had given them to mend their clothes with, also one hundred cash (about fourpence); she put these into my hand and said: “Take them away; they are not mine, I stole them." She explained that she had purloined little bits of material, etc, and with them had made little stomachers, and the hundred cash was the money she had received for them.

The whole thing was of very little value, yet I did not wish her to think lightly of sin. I reminded her that Christ had saved a thief once.

The other girl said: “I have been worse than that. Do you remember, years ago, losing your silver brooch? Search was made, and it was found under Ah-Yung's pillow; everybody thought she had taken it, but I stole it, and fearing to be found out, I put it there."

I did feel indignant and asked how she could stand by and see me punish an innocent child. I was so grieved I scarce knew what to say, but felt the first thing was to put this right with the one who had suffered.

Assembling the whole school and calling the little one to me I asked if she remembered my having punished her a few years before for stealing a brooch?

The child did not remember anything about it. I tried to refresh her memory, but it was no use, she had completely forgotten the circumstance. I told her how grieved I was that I had accused her, but had done so ignorantly; it was nevertheless a wrong, and in presence of the school I asked her to forgive me.

Quite a number of little eyes twinkled that morning; it was the first time their teacher had to confess to them her wrong-doing, and they rather enjoyed it. I then told the guilty girl that I had made all the reparation I could, and it was for her to find out in what way *she* could repair her fault. I was pleased afterwards to hear that she had given the little girl the whole of her month's money in compensation, but that the child generously returned half.

In a few days those three were clearly and distinctly converted, and in three weeks afterwards three more. One girl had already left the school to be married, and was still unsaved. As soon as the others were converted themselves they began in earnest to pray for this one; I was delighted when they asked me to join them in prayer.

The following Sunday one of the newly converted girls took the opportunity to speak to her, and told her how we were praying she might be saved. She answered carelessly, "It is no use, my heart is cold and hard. I do not seem even to care to be saved."

The following Saturday they asked if, in company with another Christian, they might visit her; and on their return they almost rushed into my study, calling out breathlessly,

"Sy-Mo, our eldest sister is saved." My husband just coming in, and hearing only the last word, called, "Wait, I want to hear too."

They then told us that the Sunday before, after the services, she had gone home in such heaviness of heart, and asked the Lord why she, the eldest of the number, should be so hard of heart? She said, while she prayed, light broke upon her, and she believed her sins were washed away.

She was baptized some months afterwards, but I am sorry to say she has not turned out to be a satisfactory Christian. Her husband, though a believer, is somewhat trying in temper, and want of harmony at home has led to coldness on the part of both. Since then there have been periodical revivals, at which time three, four, or five have been converted; and only three have left the school unsaved - for these we still pray.

During the second gracious revival amongst the girls, which took place in about two or three years after the first, when four more were converted, our coolie's wife was also saved.

He had come to us almost destitute, but with diligent work and carefulness he saved enough to get a wife, and as he had no home for her, he asked if she might live in his room for a few months, to which I consented.

She was a young girl, only fifteen, quiet and diligent, and the six months turned into many years, for they are still here with their five children, the three eldest in our schools. For about three years this young woman seemed very indifferent to the Gospel. She attended the services because she lived inside, and all were expected to do so; but at this time she ·became deeply concerned about sin, and one day, while in the act of washing clothes, it seemed as though a horror of darkness came over her. She left her work, went to Mrs. Lili, and begged her to pray that God would forgive her sins.

For two or three days she continued in an anxious state of soul, and then, yielding herself to Christ, she rejoiced in the knowledge of salvation.

In 1873, Mr. Jackson was married in Ningbo, and in due time brought his young wife to Wenzhou. We had by that time got possession of the three lower rooms as well as the three upper, and for some months they lived with us.

Mrs. Jackson's ill-health, however, called them away to Taizhou, and later on to Ningbo, and when they returned, nearly a year after, they were able to rent a house in another part of the city.

It was a great comfort to have another lady here, and we had no small fellowship one with another. They had to leave again and again for ill-health, but when it became necessary for us to take a furlough, they willingly took the responsibility of the boys' and girls' school; and the little church which had been formed. Mrs. Jackson died in September, 1878, leaving a little girl only nine days old.

The boys' school had given a good deal of encouragement, not so much in the numbers converted as the character of the converts; and at this time Die-chang and two others were preachers.

Mr. Stott, writing a little earlier, says,

Si-nüe is now nineteen years of age, and is at present acting teacher, as I have lent the school-teacher to Mr. Jackson to assist him in his difficulties.

Si-nüe is a smart lad, a good scholar, and understands the Scriptures well, but I hardly expect him to equal Tsiu-die-chang (who is now in charge of the station at Bing-yie as a preacher). He speaks at times with almost burning earnestness, enough to persuade anyone of the truth.

Si-nüe is bashful and proud, and needs very careful treatment, but there is a good deal of capital material in him. I have heard him several times in hot discussions with literary men. He can patter off the native classics glibly, and turn many passages against their silly notions with biting power.

A younger boy, Z-nüe, is nearly sixteen years of age, has been a member of the church about three years, and has all through behaved in a Christ-like manner. He is highly esteemed by the members for his consistent life. He is very quiet, but ever ready, and seldom fails to establish himself in the good graces of the people he speaks to. I expect him to be a successful evangelist.

Often when school is over, instead of going to amuse himself with the others, he has gone out with a bundle of books and tracts to the crowded thoroughfares to sell. Would that they were more deeply taught by the Spirit of God, and lived nearer to the fountain of all heat and light and love.

A letter from Si-nüe written to a friend mentioned before may prove interesting. Translated by Mr. Stott,

In the year of grace 1874, first moon.

Because I have formerly heard that for a long time you have been writing letters to Wenzhou to inquire about the welfare of the boys; but we have hardly courage to receive your messages, for we are unworthy of them, but your kindness and love abound, it is beyond our understanding.

Not only this, but many beautiful pictures you have sent for us. All who have seen them admire them.

Your kindness is deep as the sea and heavy as the hills. The boys would like to go to your place and thank you personally before your face, but the way is long, seas and hills and impassable barriers intervene, therefore we are unable to come. Also we are so unworthy, that it would be presumption in us to appear before you.

To speak of the pictures, some of them are hung in the schoolroom, some in the dining-hall, and some new ones are in the hands of a paper-hanger being done. Also there is hanging up a map of the world.

At present, there are sixteen boys in the school and we read various books, including the native classics, but the Scriptures are the textbook for morning and evening worship.

We are born with stupid minds, and our bodies are very lazy, therefore we do not know much. In our daily habits we are not diligent, we ought to hang our heads down and feel ashamed.

To speak of the church, there have not been many added for a long time, but there are a few inquiring. At present, although there is little fruit, if the Holy Spirit were only in the heart of every one who believes, the time might soon come when we should see a great increase, thirty, sixty, or a hundredfold.

I have used this small piece of paper to thank you, and pay our respects to yourself, your brothers, and all your father's house. Many things I have not made plain to you, for my composition is despicable. I only ask you not to despise it. At present let this suffice, I will write you longer at another time. May the glory of the Triune God be upon you, world without end.

P.S: This is the new year, so I will add a word more. We have heard that you have a Sunday school. How many scholars have you? We know that if you teach them anything it will be the Word of God, which is incomparably the best. I ask if you would, instead of me, salute all your scholars and convey to them a message. 'You have been born in a country where there are no idols; you have not been defiled by them like us, their defilement has gone into us like dye into the fabric.' Although you are free of that sin, do not forget that you are the seed of Adam, in that you are the same as us; if you do not trust in the precious blood of Jesus Christ, our middle man, all is vain and useless.

The Holy Book says, 'Believe on the Lord Jesus Christ and thou shalt be saved,' but 'he that believeth not shall be condemned.' Do lay these words to heart. Would that all of you would earnestly pray God to interest the minds of many of your countrymen to come to China and point out the way to heaven. Revered master, no more, but all the boys in the school join in salutations to you.

Written by Si-nüe.

Up to that time much seed had been sown, but little fruit gathered in. We had evangelised in nearly all the villages around the city. Frequently we would start in the morning, taking lunch with us, preaching in various villages; my husband gathering the men, and I the women, under some spreading tree. Many heard, but, alas, few believed that Jesus was the only Saviour.

But is it not always so? We need constantly to remember the promise that "He that goeth forth weeping, bearing precious seed, shall doubtless come again with rejoicing, bringing his sheaves with him." It is for us to observe the conditions "precious seed," the Word of God; "weeping hearts" longing for souls, that will not be satisfied without fruit.

As the result of our first ten years' labour, a little church of only eighteen or twenty was formed; how meagre apparently the return for so much labour. We had often in those days to assure ourselves of His faithfulness, who has said, "In due season ye shall reap if ye faint not." But besides this mere handful of Christians there were many hopeful inquirers, and during our absence of eighteen months thirty-seven were baptized on profession of their faith.

As the result of our first ten years' labour, a little church of only eighteen or twenty was formed; how meagre apparently the return for so much labour.

CHAPTER 6

Lack Ye Anything?

And He said unto them, Lacked ye anything? And they said, Nothing." Luke 22:35

On the 1st of April, 1877, Wenzhou became an open port. It was a new thing for us to see a steamer in the river, and we had a feeling almost of intrusion when we went on the hill and met other foreigners there. The state of my health in that year rendered it necessary to take a furlough to England, and we left by the first trading steamer that came to Wenzhou.

Mr. Stott had been over eleven years in China, and his health being good, he at first thought of sending me home while he remained at his post. Mr. Taylor, however, kindly suggested he should take me, and that suggestion was carried out.

At that time the little girls were beginning to grow up, and we felt keenly the need of a separate house for them. The state of the mission funds did not encourage us to look to them for the rather large sum that would be needed to build a girls' school-house.

We took our need to the Lord, told Him if that work had to be carried on a home must be provided for them. We decided to make no appeal of any kind, not even to mention our need publicly, but that we should tell our private friends of our desire, and leave the rest to God.

We told Hudson Taylor of our plan, and said we thought £250 would be needed; he said he thought not less than £300 would suffice. We had asked the Lord for £250, but we told Him about the £300, and if it was needed, to send us that sum.

When we returned to China in the autumn of the following year we had received unsolicited £304, besides having spent £10 on school materials; it was another of the "exceeding abundantly" which the Lord has ever loved to give us. We had decided together that we should limit our own expenses to the sums received from the mission for our own support, and whatever gifts were given to us should be put to the school fund.

During this time we had some very singular experiences. When in Ireland my husband was asked to address a few Christians who lived in a quiet out-of-the-way village. The people were poor, they had nothing to give but their prayers; but Mr. Stott felt prayer was a mightier power than money, so he went seeking to interest these godly people.

The meeting was held in a farmhouse; not more than twenty were present, but they were deeply interested in all they heard. When the meeting was over, one and another pressed up to shake hands with the missionary, and one woman, with tears in her eyes, pressed a coin in his hand, he putting it into a pocket where there was no other money. When he retired to his room he looked to see what the coin might be, and was deeply touched to find it one "halfpenny."

He felt it was like the "widow's mite," and at once knelt down to ask God to bless her gift. He then entered in his book, "A poor woman unknown, a halfpenny."

The next day when he returned to me he said, "I was deeply humbled, and had to confess to God that if I had had only a halfpenny to give I should have been too much ashamed to have put it into the hand; she had much more faith and love than I." Then he added, "Do you know God seems to have shown me that He is going to send £50."

I answered, "Oh, I have not faith for that, but according to your faith, be it unto you." We then knelt down together and asked God again to bless that woman who had so nobly given all she could, and was not ashamed of the smallness of the sum.

The next day, we went to spend a few days with a friend in another part of the country. The day after, while the lady and I were out for a drive, our host came to the room where my husband was writing, and said, "God has told me to give you this money for your work."

He put down a bundle of notes and left the room. On counting them Mr. Stott found there were just £50! It was entered as the next donation to the halfpenny, and up to this time we had never received more than £5 in a single gift.

We then went on to Dublin, where we were hospitably entertained by a dear Christian couple, and while sitting by the fire recounting the Lord's wonderful dealings with us, my husband mentioned the incident of the halfpenny and £50. He then added, much to my confusion, "And I have the same strong conviction that God is sending me £5."

When we retired to rest I asked why he had said such a thing. "It was as good as asking, and no doubt next day when we are leaving £5 will be given." He answered, "Oh, I never thought of that, but of course I can explain and refuse."

Next day, as I expected, a cheque for £5 was handed. My husband refused to touch it, expressed his regret for having mentioned his conviction in the way he did: it was all right to tell of what God had done, but what He was going to do seemed too like a hint, and if he wished to spare his feelings he must not ask him to accept this.

Our host replied, "That £5 was given to me two days ago by another. It is not my money at all. My wife and I laughed when we went upstairs; it is no use trying to cheat you, for God evidently tells you beforehand."

These are a few of the remarkable ways in which God supplied all our needs very abundantly. Our visit home was productive of much interest and prayer; I had specially asked that friends would plead that some suitable woman might be converted who would be a real help in work amongst others, for up to that time we had only one Christian woman, and she was over seventy.

I felt the drawback of being alone, and longed for such a helper. Little did we think that, while they prayed, God was working out His own plans in that direction.

We arrived back in Wenzhou on the last day of 1878. Two days afterwards I was asked to visit two women who were interested in the truth and wanted to see me.

Mrs. Liu, our former Bible-woman; her son, now labouring in Tai-chow; his wife, a former school-girl; and their three children, the eldest of whom is converted.

Oh! What good news! Two women interested in the grand story of the Cross. Of course I went without delay, and was delighted to find them not only interested, but truly converted.

They told me that one of our members, a firewood seller, had every time he brought their wood, sat down to tell them of God and His Christ.

At first they were indifferent, but by and by they began to long for his coming, that they might hear more and more.

Afterwards they were visited by schoolboys, and others who could teach them. One of these women mentioned how in former years she had closed her door when she saw me coming up the street, lest I should try to get into her house as I did others; but added, "Now I am longing for you to teach me the Bible."

This lady, Mrs. Liu, was of a refined literary family, and when young was married to a man of wealth; but alas, he, his father, and two brothers were opium smokers, and as they had no business of any kind, the property grew less and less each year, until the death of her husband.

After paying his debts she had but a remnant of property left, not enough to keep herself and son - at that time a lad of seven or eight. After her husband's death she gave herself up very largely to the worship of idols, but in that she found no comfort for her weary spirit.

The other woman was a working man's wife, Mrs. Oae, very bright and earnest. Her husband was bitterly opposed to her being a Christian, and would not allow her to attend any services, nor would he consent to any Christian visiting her in her home; but as these two women lived in opposite sides of the same house, he could not prevent our going to Mrs. Liu's, nor his wife from listening.

I at once began a Bible-class each Wednesday afternoon in Mrs. Liu's house. Neither had ever attended a Christian service-one prevented by her husband, the other too much ashamed to be seen outside. Now I look back with great joy to the time spent teaching those women. Their hearts were indeed opened, and eagerly they drank in the precious words of life. Week by week they repeated almost word by word the lesson of the week before, and it was wonderful to see their rapid growth in grace.

One Wednesday I went as usual, but found Mrs. Liu was not at home. Mrs. Oae told me that her mother-in-law had died two days before, and that she had been called to the funeral ceremonies. She left a message that we were to pray for her, as she did not know what to do under such circumstances.

So that afternoon, instead of our Bible lesson, we spent the time in prayer, that God would keep His child in the midst of difficulty and sore temptation.

The next two or three days I was very anxious and much in prayer for her. I feared the effect of all the deadening influences of idolatry. I wondered if she would have courage to confess Christ before her proud literary relations.

Three days afterwards she came to see me, and the first glance of her told all was well, for her face fairly beamed. Her first words were, "It is wonderful, wonderful! God stood by me all the time."

She then told me that when being carried in her chair she was greatly perplexed about what to do, and could only cry, "God, help me to glorify Thee." When she arrived and saw all her relatives going through the idolatrous ceremonies, her heart smote her, and she felt she must confess Christ.

She called them together and told them how that, since they had last met, a wonderful change had come over her. She had heard of a true and living God, who could wash away her sins and make her more happy than any earthly treasure could; that the knowledge of an everlasting home in heaven was more than earthly gain, and that though she and her son were the nearest relatives, and had a right to most of the property of the deceased, yet she could not offend God by performing the necessary ancestral rights.

Her son was young, but she hoped he, too, would become a Christian by and by, and that he must not undertake those rites either.

She therefore gave up all claim to the property, and would leave it with themselves to give what they thought right, on the understanding that she and her son would be forever free from ancestral worship.

She also added that they began to ask what kind of a religion it was that could make her do such a thing, and so, she said, "for three days I have been doing little else but telling them of Jesus, and just before coming away God let me know I had glorified Him, for I heard one of my relatives say, 'That must be a good religion, for if you searched the city through you could not find another who would give up property like that.'"

I am ashamed to say that they only gave her the sixteenth part of what she ought to have had, but with that she got a written statement that at her decease, none of them were to interfere with her funeral, or perform idolatrous rites.

For many years she has been a faithful and valuable helper in the work here. Her son was trained for several years under Dr. Douthwaite, and there converted. He is now doing medical work in the city of Taizhou.

Mrs. Oae, who had been prevented by her husband from making any public confession of her faith, began to feel an earnest desire to be baptized. I counselled waiting upon the Lord in the matter, hoping that her husband might give consent.

One day on going to the class she told me, with a beaming face, that her husband was going away the next day to do some work in the country, and would be away till the following Monday or Tuesday. She said, "For three days I have been praying that God would open up my way to be baptized and this is His answer."

I reminded her that it was very cold weather (we baptized by immersion, and the baptistry was an open one in our courtyard), and asked if she was not afraid.

She answered, "Oh, no! God has given me this opportunity, and if I do not take it He may never give me another." I was a little doubtful about her taking this step without the knowledge and consent of her husband; but she seemed so certain that God had given her a chance not to be thrown away, that I could but be silent.

On Saturday evening she came out for the first time in her life to a Christian service, and gave such a testimony to the power and preciousness of the blood of Jesus Christ as quite astonished the little group of Christians.

She was unanimously accepted by them for baptism the following morning, after which she joined in our communion service. How strange it must all have seemed to her. She had never seen memorials of Christ's broken body before, but her Spirit-taught soul greatly rejoiced at being able to join with others in thus publicly remembering her Lord.

After the afternoon service she returned home and had only just laid aside her outdoor garments, when to her astonishment in walked her husband. He saw from her appearance she had been out, and questioned her, when she boldly acknowledged she had been to the chapel. He grumbled something about being disgraced in the eyes of his fellow-workmen by his wife going after a foreign religion, but on the whole took it very quietly, much to her relief.

This dear woman led a bright, earnest, consistent life for some years. She was one from whom I had hoped much, but one Sunday morning in 1888, while we were in England, she died quite suddenly just as she was preparing to go out to the service.

About this time (1879), another bright woman was converted. She impressed me so much by her intelligence and ability to receive the truth, that for about two years I went regularly to her house one afternoon each week to teach her.

Work in China in the earlier years had to be done among the ones and twos. For two years I carried on two classes a week, one composed of two women, the other only of one, but it was well-repaid labour, for the lives of these three were bright and shining witnesses for Christ.

This woman, Ah-Chang-na, was very poor, yet had a joy in giving to the Lord that surprised us all; for when we began our native women's missionary band, she was one of the most regular contributors. Day by day, from her housekeeping money, she would put aside one cash for God, and often in the middle of the month she would bring the money to me to keep for her, lest in her extreme poverty she might be tempted to use it.

She had a young family, and could do little beyond her household duties; but if she earned a little money with her own hands, she always gave one-half of it to God as a thanks-offering.

I remember, one New Year's time, at our native missionary meeting, telling the women God would be no man's debtor, and that whenever we from a true heart desired to spread the knowledge of His name and gave what we could ill afford, He would be sure to reward. I looked to this woman for confirmation, and said, "Ah-Chang-na, you are one of the poorest of us, yet you have given to God this year more than ever before, and more than any of the others; will you tell us how God has dealt with you - has it been harder for you to pass this year than formerly?" I asked this in faith, yet tremblingly, not knowing what the answer would be. With a beaming face she declared, before all, that at the end of the year, after paying off her little debts, she had one dollar left upon which to enter a new year.

She said, "never in my whole life have I had one dollar to begin the New Year with before." We did praise God for that blessed testimony, and often has it been quoted since. This dear woman, too, passed away in 1888, while we were at home in England.

It seemed to us so sad, that two out of our three brightest and best Christians should be called away so near each other, and at a time when they seemed more than ever needed.

Before they were called home, however, they saw a goodly band of women gathered out of darkness into God's wondrous light.

I must say, Ah-Chang-na was a Christian who never gave me an hour's anxiety, so consistent and bright was her life throughout. She had much power in prayer, and literally prayed her husband and mother into the kingdom.

We had a meeting amongst the women every Thursday afternoon, especially to pray for unsaved relatives, and this dear woman often broke down while pleading for others. It will be interesting to note that during the first few years of its existence, no fewer than four husbands, and seven children, of our praying women were brought to the Lord.

It was out of this prayer-meeting grew our Missionary Band. I was a little perplexed to know how to get them out of the narrow groove of themselves and circumstances, into interest in and sympathy for others. I knew it would be a benefit to their own souls to do something for those around. We began in a very simple way, contributing what we could once a month, to enable one of their own number to go out as a Bible-woman.

Mrs. Liu was chosen, and, as long as health permitted, faithfully represented them. This Missionary Band was a great blessing to the women themselves; the missionary information I was able to give them, month by month, stirred up their hearts and interest and stimulated prayer, besides producing a self-denying spirit in the matter of giving.

This Missionary Band has now (1895) been in existence for ten years. Of course it has grown with our Christian women, and for some years they have almost entirely supported their own Bible-women.

Our schoolgirls, though having no money of their own, were most desirous of helping in this effort; a barber had to be called twice a month to shave the heads of the little girls according to the Chinese custom, and one day the elder girls asked if I would allow them to do the head shaving. I asked why; they replied, "We do want to help with the Bible-women, and we thought if we could do the work instead of the barber, the money might go to the missionary fund."

I was only too glad to accede to their wish, and the effort has been continued ever since by those, who in turn, become the elder girls of the school.

In the summer of 1879, we began building the girls' school for which God had so graciously supplied the funds. At first we intended only to build a house large enough for a school, but felt led to build instead a double house, where the school could be at one end and our rooms at the other, so that I might be in a better position to superintend them; and also that the native house we had lived in for ten years might be available for a married couple whom we hoped would soon join us. With our enlarged plans we knew we should need more money, but as this seemed the right thing, and God had proved Himself so faithful in the past, we felt sure He would supply unasked all that was needed.

The house was to be built by piecework, and we determined to go on only as far as we had money in hand. We paid men and materials week by week. Twice we thought we should have to tell the head workmen to withdraw their men for a time, and twice fresh supplies came before that was necessary. The whole was finished without a single day's stoppage for want of funds, and of course without one penny of debt. We had to wait a little time before we could put up the necessary outhouses; but they, too, were provided in answer to believing prayer.

These buildings, native houses, chapel, etc, were all destroyed in the riot of 1884.

CHAPTER 7

LETTERS FROM THE FIELD

"If any man will come after Me, let him deny himself, and take up his cross daily, and follow Me." Luke 9:23

As soon as building operations were finished, regular itinerations were again commenced, mostly by Mr. Stott alone, as the girls' and women's work occupied my time more and more. He had to make occasional visits to Chaozhou, which was then an out-station from Wenzhou, as well as to Bing-yie and Dong-ling, where the work was growing steadily.

Referring to a few of these journeys, Mr. Stott writes,

Jan. 1880.

My dear Mr. A.-

When yours came to hand I felt conscience-stricken. There was no time to reply, as I was just starting for Chaozhou. I had to go up the river ninety miles in a small miserable boat. The weather was very cold, a bleak north wind, sleet and hail driving in our teeth. The boat cover was in such bad condition that I had to compel the boatman to get a new one; and by urging and coaxing I reached my destination in a little less than three days.

On both sides of the river there are many villages and small towns which have not yet been visited by any Christian.

I trust I may be able to give them the offer of salvation 'ere long. Every one travelling in China and seeing the countless towns and villages, with their thousands of inhabitants, could not remain unmoved. They are born, live, and die, generation after generation, seeking nothing higher than to have enough to eat and wear, and leave a small portion for their children.

On arriving there, it was no better than the boat for comfort - the hail came through the roof and left no place dry; the room where my bed was had only two sides to it, and I can assure you the ventilation was perfect! However, the day following, I got some boards and a carpenter and closed it in a bit, but then all the light I had was through the tiles.

The silver lining in my cloud was a small stove, which I had brought with me, and I assure you the warmth from it was grateful to a degree. I remained there four days, and tried to strengthen the hearts of those who are looking forward to the house of many mansions in the skies."

"More recently I have been to Bing-yie, south of Wenzhou, and spent a very happy time, having met thirty persons all interested and more or less instructed in the truth.

There are ten or twelve more in the same country, but as they live a long way off I did not see them. Ten of the best out of the thirty were invited to come to the city and spend a little time with us in Bible study.

There are a good many inquirers in the district where I go tomorrow, and perhaps three or four may be accepted.

Last Lord's day, a woman came about sixteen miles, and got one of the Christians to introduce her to us. She wanted to be 'baptized and made a disciple of Jesus.' After talking to her for some time, we found that she and her husband had been taught by one of the native Christians, who sometimes visit their village on business. Their idols were thrown away some months ago, and the husband had been to the chapel a good many times, but never made himself known.

We expect Mr. and Mrs. Douthwaite, of our Mission, soon. They have been six or seven years in China and he has practised medicine, I believe very successfully. We hope that blessing may follow his medical work here, but he is far from strong and it is doubtful whether the damp climate of this district will suit his health.

Mrs. Stott and I do a little in the practice of homeopathy. Mrs. Stott got a nice chest from Mr. R., whom we met in your brother's house at Pinner. Mr. R. also gave me a small bottle of a special preparation called 'Neuraline,' said to be an instant cure for sciatica. I tried it once when an attack was coming on, and in half an hour the pain was gone. I left the bottle in the bedroom, and when the old woman went to make the bed she was attracted by its fragrant, pleasing smell; afterwards, on meeting the old withered beauty, I could not make out what she had been anointing herself with, as she really distilled fragrance at every step, and, as the cook remarked, 'You could hear the fragrance of her all over the yard.' But when I discovered my loss, I felt as an Irishman at Limerick once expressed himself, “An' shure it was a little riled that I was, sur.”

I hope you are not thinking too highly of the China Inland Mission. It is not perfect, nor ever will be as long as I am connected with it; but it is as near perfection as any mission I know of.

I am glad you are no enemy to system and order in connection with service for our Master; if there was no organisation or system I do not think the C.I.M. could do as good or as much work as it does, and instead of less, I think we need more of it.

Did it ever strike you that some of these good men who are so afraid of system in the Lord's work are yet very systematic in their habits?

Take, for instance, their systematic reading and study of God's Word, meeting with kindred spirits for prayer, etc, at stated hours and places, which many of them would not forego for any worldly gain.

To give an illustration of this kind of inconsistency, I met in —-- a good man and pillar of the church of —-- and we talked about missions in general and the C.l.M. in particular. He liked the mission very well, but was afraid it was running too much into system. He complained that a council was now formed in London, Hudson Taylor was Bishop in China, and every member was under his thumb; that he used his power rather unsparingly, and perhaps it was a mistake that he should have so much power over the brethren.

My part, of course, was to defend as best I could; then the conversation turned upon our own work in particular. I told him much of what had been done, and more that was still undone, and the conclusion he came to was, that one man could not do well the work on hand.

To ease his mind I informed him that Hudson Taylor had promised me help as soon as circumstances would allow; a young man, or perhaps two, would join me soon.

So far, so good. Did I know either of the young men?

I could not say that I did. Then he said, It was most important that a proper understanding should exist, to begin with; the work was already established, and if some young man or men were to join who would not work willingly on the lines already laid down, but upset here and overturn there, they would do more harm than good, and damage the work of the Lord by unskilled hands.

I told him it was understood by all parties that the new-comers must work on the lines already laid down, and were not at liberty to tear up old or lay down new ones. He felt relieved and happy then, and said, 'That was just as it should be,' but the dear man did not see that he had cut away the foundation from his own remarks about Hudson Taylor having control over the members.

I think it is a scriptural thing for the younger to be in submission to the elder. Yea, more than that, if it is not put into practice, confusion will be the result, as is often but too plainly seen."

"Two Sundays ago we had eight persons baptized here, who gave us much comfort and hope, which I pray may not be disappointed. Others, by God's grace, seem to be pressing forward.

For some time past, I think the Spirit of God has been helping me in making the way of salvation through Christ clear; for oh, it is hard for them to understand the precious truths, their minds are so dark.

Yesterday was the Lord's day, and I think His Spirit was with us in power. At evening prayer the word spoken seemed to touch every heart, and at the close I asked two of the brethren to lead us in prayer.

One of the Christians prayed first. Then an inquirer began for the first time. Inquirers are not expected to pray, but I did not like to stop him; he is an elderly, grey-haired man, venerable in appearance and highly esteemed by all who know him.

At first I feared his attempt would cause an explosion among the young folk, but to their credit be it said they behaved better than your scholars would have done. I think his simple earnestness over-awed every one, and at the end there was such a hearty 'Amen' from all present as if they really meant to thank God for opening another mouth to worship Him. This old gentleman and two of his neighbours had been constant attendants for about a year. There is no doubt that they like the gospel, but whether they are all subjects of the saving grace of God it would be hard to say; but I think the one who prayed last night is.

It is very good of the Lord to give us even a little success. We are so unworthy of it, but He saves in spite of our unworthiness.

Thirty-four in all have been gathered in since our return a year ago. It is much to thank God for, but what are they among the many thousands who hear as though they heard not? Many listen for a long time before they ever dream that any object of worship can or ought to exist besides what they already possess.

(A little later he writes)

Since writing you last we have accepted and baptized ten persons; most have been coming to the services one, two, or three years.

Last Lord's day the chapel was full, and in the afternoon Mrs. Stott had thirty women in her class; she calls this a class for teaching them the Scriptures, but I fancy there is some preaching goes on as well. I have not been there to see, but I think most of her meetings contain more or less of the preaching element; but as long as souls are saved and God's blessing rests on them, I think it would be a mistake for her to stop, even if the Archbishop of Canterbury were to condemn her. The Lord has given His seal, and that is what we look, long, pray, and give thanks for.

This year, 1881, more have been gathered into the church than any one year since the work began, but during this time a few have been put under discipline: one man long in fellowship, and who had a good deal of influence and had been the means of bringing a goodly number under the sound of the Word, has departed from the faith and godliness, and since his suspension has been behaving in a very unbecoming manner. These things are our trials, but the work is the Lord's, not ours, and He will bring into His kingdom all that are His.

These things are our trials, but the work is the Lord's, not ours, and He will bring into His kingdom all that are His.

Satan seems to have greater power than ever in hurting the saints of God, by causing many to turn from the faith and accept unsound doctrine. It all points to the fact that the Lord is at hand. I sometimes so long for His appearing, because our whole hope for the Church and the world is centred in His coming to take the government of the world into His own hands; the sadness and suffering all around is great indeed, the misery day by day is appalling.

As an instance, only last month a poor man, in a country village, whose daughter was ill and supposed to be dying, had, according to custom, lighted two candles, put them in paper lanterns and hung one at the head and the other at the foot of the bed.

He then fastened both the door and window and went on to the top of the house to call back his daughter's spirit. He stood and called long, and during the time one of the candles fell down and set the bed on fire before the people of the house knew it, and then they could not get in. By the time they reached the fire, it had taken such a hold that six houses were destroyed before it could be conquered.

The man's daughter was burnt to death, as well as a woman in another house; and a young man was so severely injured in trying to save his family and property that he died the next day.

More than half the fires that take place in China result from idolatry or from opium smoking.

More than half the fires that take place in China result from idolatry or from opium smoking.

I have lately come in from the Dong-ling station. I had a good time on the whole, but a serious fever prevented me from extending my journey.

Concerning the four persons baptized, one or two things were a little remarkable. One lad was about fourteen years of age, (I have only once baptized one so young before and he is now twenty-two years of age) and went into the water with them and performed the rite. I only hope this lad may turn out as well.

Two others were husband and wife.

The fourth, a very nice young woman and daughter of two of our Christians. She is married into a family who are opposed to the truth, and has a great deal to bear for Christ's sake, and seems to bear it cheerfully. She was engaged to be married into this family before she or her parents heard the Gospel.

(In after years, this young woman led her husband to the truth, and gained the goodwill of her other relatives, so that her mother-in-law, though never a Christian, was changed from a persecutor into a friend. I remember when visiting there, the mother-in-law spoke gratefully of her daughter's goodness.)

I thank God and take courage, but must confess that every time there is a baptism I am filled almost as much with fear as with joy. Fear – lest I should have committed any mistake, or that Satan may lead them away into sin, thus causing shame and dishonour to God and His Word.

Here in the city we baptized three persons last week, and hope to receive more soon. Some of them have been giving us much comfort. They are mostly from Mrs. Stott's Bible-class.

The Lord has been and still is blessing her efforts among the women, many of whom seem to accept the truth more readily than their husbands, and also walk more consistently than the rougher sex. Indeed some of our best Christians are women, and Mrs. Stott has often told me that at their prayer-meetings they seem to unburden the very secret of their souls to the Lord, and confess their sins, temptations, and failures with an openness and earnestness unknown at home.

Some of our best Christians are women. They seem to unburden the very secret of their souls to the Lord, and confess their sins, temptations, and failures with an openness and earnestness unknown at home.

They often pray for twenty or twenty-five minutes at a time. They begin with their hearts full almost to bursting, and are not happy till they have told all their story (not the half); and having told it, their faces beam with delight, and they go on their way strengthened with faith, hope, and love.

Prayer is very real to them, and the answers just as real. At the same time there is a good deal of persecution. At one place some have been badly beaten, and at another they are afraid almost daily that their houses will be pulled down and themselves maltreated.

I think I told you that one poor woman who was ill-used last year never recovered from the effects of the cruelty she was subjected to, and has lately died.

At another place an old man had his house set on fire twice; he was at last driven away, and is now ill, not expected to live.

Another is a very sad case; a brother's wife died, and the neighbours would not allow him to bury her without going through all the heathen rites for the dead, nor would they allow him to bring the coffin into the village, nor carry the corpse out. Several of the members went to visit him, but they were beaten, one of them very badly. At last our brother escaped, and ran here as if for his life. We had a good deal of trouble in arranging the matter and 'ere then the corpse was much decayed. Then the neighbours insisted upon the other Christians performing the rites, and on their refusal they were beaten, and their hands bound and tied to the bed over the decaying corpse, while the heathen neighbours went through the rites; they then brought in the coffin, and tied two of the Christians to it by their tails.

I hope the trouble is over now, and that we have strengthened our position.

It seems impossible to advance one step without stirring up the devil, and having to maintain our ground inch by inch. I pray this may be a real blow at the supremacy of his power in that place.

There are a few inquirers there, and when Mr. Jackson went up to see about the burying of the brother's wife, all the Christians and inquirers came to see him, except one young man who was tied up to a post by his father lest he should catch the 'Jesus disease.' He had been too late in tying him up, for he caught the disease more than a year ago, and now the father finds it difficult to cure him.

One young man was tied up to a post by his father lest he should catch the 'Jesus disease.' He had been too late in tying him up, for he caught the disease more than a year ago, and now the father finds it difficult to cure him.

There are others I could tell you of, suffering the loss of their little all for Christ's sake.

Since I wrote you last the Lord has been blessing us. One Lord's day we had ten persons baptized and last Sunday three. There is a spirit of inquiry abroad in many places, but we are much hampered for want of native assistants. The people are willing to hear, but we have hardly any one to tell them the way of salvation. We have been especially crying to God about this matter. We have few in the church fitted for teaching others, and it takes a long time to train so as to fit them for this work. Our hope and confidence is in God. He has provided many things for us, He is able to provide this also."

I came in from the country yesterday; had a rainy, disagreeable time, and some unpleasant things to do. Satan seems to break loose every now and again, and do all the mischief he can to the Christians. One man who steadily refused to contribute to the support of the heathen temple had half his standing corn cut, and what was left was trampled, so that he suffered a serious loss.

Others have had their farming implements broken to pieces, been denied the use of the public road, and annoyed in many ways, for they are adepts in the art of petty persecution.

It is surely a testing time for us all, and makes me long for the time when our Lord Himself shall come and save His own out of the hand of the wicked.

July 1, 1884.

This is quarter day, when accounts have to be made up and dispatched, a great deal of pastoral work has claimed my attention.

My dear wife is feeling weighed down with extra work, and I give her an hour's help daily. We are hard worked certainly, but thanks be to God, His presence is with us, sustaining and helping.

Last Saturday evening I was up until 11pm examining sixteen candidates for baptism. Eleven were accepted and baptized on Sunday morning, and afterwards sat down at the Lord's table.

Some of those deferred will soon be received, I think, as they were put off only until some family matters could be arranged. This year we have already received thirty two and I hope God will give us a great many more before the end. I long to get into that state of soul-communion with God in which the good man is supposed to be, when 'all he doeth shall prosper.'"

The rumours of war so near us have given me a good deal of extra work. Many of the Christians in distant places are having rough times; the heathen are persecuting them fiercely, but as yet no blows have been struck.

The Romanists are getting it worse than we, and a rupture has taken place, but I have not heard the details. The Chinese are not so enlightened as to make much if any distinction between one foreigner and another. Here they distinguish our nationalities by our religion:

Protestants are British and are very bad - they produce the opium.

Romanists are French, they are even more abominable and ought to be exterminated.

Such is the expressed feeling of many. Our most southern station is near the border of Fujian, and with hostilities going on so near, there is much to try them. There is also a great deal of excitement in the city, and some days we can hardly walk out without being reminded of the dislike with which many regard us. They will sometimes get behind us and make a harsh whirring noise like sharpening a knife, and if they can draw our attention will take their fan and make a significant slash at their necks, and then disappear as soon as they can. But if matters do not get worse we will be thankful.

The Lord reigneth, and our confidence is in Him.

I do not go out more than I can help, and so far have been treated with respect. The mandarins seem in earnest in trying to keep the peace, and have issued a good proclamation.

I am told they have soldiers parading the streets and secret spies loitering about, and any detected stirring up the people are taken to the Yamen and soundly thrashed. What we all fear is bands of robbers, who are always on the alert to embrace the first opportunity of plunder that presents itself. But our souls are in God's mighty hand, and our bodies too; and He will take care of us till our work is done. We are more anxious about our friends in the far interior, and daily pray that they may be kept in peace; we trust their distance from the seat of hostilities may be some protection to them.

I propose to send Mrs. Stott to Shanghai for a month, when the cool weather comes. She has had heavy work during the summer and is purposing taking in a number of women during the winter for Bible instruction that they may be the more intelligent witnesses for our Lord and Saviour. There is a great difference between a well-taught Christian and an ill-taught one - I mean in their being able to bear witness for Jesus.

If we can only give all the native converts a good hold of the Scriptures, we might in a great measure dispense with native preachers."

CHAPTER 8

Why Do The Heathen Rage?

"Why do the heathen rage, and the people imagine a vain thing?" Psalm 2:1

There was at this time a war between France and China, and during the summer of that year the French had bombarded Fuzhou, sunk several gunboats, and destroyed the arsenal there.

Fuzhou was the next port south of us, and when the news came of these disasters the people were greatly alarmed. The excitement was increased by the officials issuing orders that each household was to provide a basket of stones, which were to be placed in ships and sunk at the mouth of the river, to block it in case the French should come here.

All July and August the excitement prevailed, and had a riot happened then we should not have been so much surprised; but things quieted down and our fears were allayed.

It was during this summer that the conversion of the six girls of which I have spoken took place. New life had brought new desires for further teaching. At the end of September, my husband insisted I should go to Shanghai for a fortnight's rest, before beginning some fresh work contemplated for the autumn. My last words were, "I can go away contented and happy, for the people are so quiet and contented again."

Little did I anticipate the blow that was to fall so soon.

On Saturday evening, October the 4th, just one week after I had left, while Mr. Soothill, of the Methodist Free Church, was conducting their usual prayer meeting, a few rowdies collected at his chapel door and noisily demanded admittance. When the door was opened they ran away.

This was repeated two or three times, and on the door being again opened, several rushed in throwing stones, and evidently bent on mischief. Someone raised the cry, "Burn the foreigners out," and almost before the words were uttered they lighted torches, and, with paraffin oil set the place in flames.

The chapel was close by the house, and Mr. SoothiII, fearing a general conflagration, went to the Yamen to beseech help. The magistrate, thinking Mr. Soothill might meet with bodily injury, refused to let him out again; but he, accompanied by some soldiers, went in the hope of quelling what had now become a serious riot.

He was told, however, he had better go back; the people were bent upon mischief, and he might get injured in the fray. His chair was, indeed, considerably battered, and, mandarin like, he thought discretion the better part of valour; and the soldiers sent to intimidate the rioters joined with them in their evil work.

When Mr. Soothill's house, chapel, and all he possessed were in ruins, they made for the Roman Catholic premises. The poor priest had a hard time of it. Frightened almost out of his senses, he lay hid for three days in the firewood house of a friendly neighbour, and was at last disguised as a chinese coolie and taken to the Yamen.

The destruction there was thorough also. The mob now seemed like tigers who had tasted blood and they determined to make a clean sweep of everything belonging to the hated foreigner. From the Roman Catholic place they went to Mr. Jackson's, of our own mission, and when they reached our chapel, only three minutes' walk from our house, Mr. Stott felt it was time to seek a place of safety.

Dr. McGowan, of the Chinese Customs, had, at great personal risk, come to Mr. Stott's help. They collected our sixteen school girls (the younger of whom had to be taken from their beds), servants, and all others within our gates, in order to seek shelter in the magistrate's Yamen.

As they went out at the back gate, the first contingent of the rioters burst in at the front and in a few moments were in possession of the place. Happily the Yamen was near, or it might have fared badly with them, for they were freely pelted with stones, one of which struck Mr. Stott's pith helmet a heavy blow, which made his hat roll on the ground, and caused him to run the gauntlet bare-headed. A moment after Dr. McGowan staggered under the blow of another, and the frightened school children, who were clinging to his coat-tails, were scattered here and there.

When they reached the Yamen several of the girls were missing. Our cook, an active, earnest man, went out in search of them, but it was the next day before the family was complete. Two or three of them spent the night in a temple courtyard, scarcely daring to breathe, lest their hiding-place should be discovered. I have said complete, but there was one dear little thing three years of age, pet of the household, who was carried off, and we never saw her again.

In a few hours the destruction was general, not only the effects of the missionaries, but also of the foreigners in the Chinese Customs employ; everything foreign was destroyed. They showed a nice discrimination, for the latter, who lived in old temples, had all their goods, furniture, etc, carried out, even partition boards and flooring which they had put down, burnt in the front yard, while the buildings were left intact.

After completing their work of destruction in the city they tried to reach the English Consulate, which is situated on a small island in the middle of the river; but the magistrate had anticipated their intention, and had ordered all boats to the other side. They tried to make a raft, but failed, and the next day the homeless refugees were escorted by a strong band to the island.

On Monday the rioters went to our country chapel in Dongling, twenty English miles away, and burnt it also to the ground. We all shared the same fate, proving that the feeling was anti-foreign, not anti-missionary. The officials acted with creditable promptness in paying the indemnity demanded by the consul, and in six weeks from the date of the riot, Mr. Stott was able to return and begin rebuilding, leaving our school children in the kind care of Dr. and Mrs. Lord, of Ningbo, who most unselfishly received them into their school, although it was at the time quite full, and kept them under the care of their own matron, Mrs. Liu, for five months, during which time we were rebuilding.

It was an anxious time. The war had upset our steamer communication, and Ningbo was blockaded. For three months we were without letters, and heard vague rumours of the bombardment of Ningbo and flight of the foreigners there, which happily proved untrue; while they, poor things, suffered also through false reports concerning us. But in all this the Lord kept our hearts resting upon Himself.

The news of Mr. Stott's arrival soon spread, and it was a great joy for pastor and people to be united once more.

In February, 1885, Mr. Stott writes,

My dear Mr. A.,

I have just finished the duties of the day, and will now indulge in the pleasure of a chat with you. You are one of my oldest friends, and that gives me licence.

I am here alone as yet, for my dear wife could not leave Shanghai owing to the death of Miss Minchin - and, indeed, I was not in a state to receive her sooner. After getting official liberty to return, I came by first steamer and at once began to search for a temporary home.

After many failures the Lord gave me success. I have bought a small house adjoining my former property, and I am now living in it in tolerable comfort. I had to pull down the ruined walls of our dear old home, and I must confess it cost me many a pang to stand by and see it done; and our dear little garden, which was such a pleasure to my wife, all disfigured, not a plant, shrub, or even a weed left.

We had a large number of flowers in pots, which were mostly thrown down the well. At every corner were signs of the most wanton destruction. Surely their mischievous ingenuity came from near the bottom of the bottomless pit. And now quiet has been restored, the mandarins are doing very little to bring the rioters to justice. Many of the native Christians have been looted of their all, and the mandarins will not even look at their petitions for redress.

Very few out of China have any idea of the weakness and corruption of the Mandarinate and their hatred of all Europeans. Those brought to justice are comforted and consoled by the mandarins telling them that they must apprehend and punish them through pressure, for the "foreign devils " are very cruel, and destitute of any mercy.

I am now rebuilding, and the girls' school will be finished next month, also the chapel at Dong-ling; our own house is some distance on, but the city chapel still lies in abeyance. Hitherto the Lord has helped me, and I do need His help, for I am poor and needy.

The British Consul has entered into the case with much spirit, and has done for every one as well as he could. Two instalments of the indemnity have been paid, and another is almost due.

I am glad to say I have found nearly all the Christians have stood firm, only one having gone back. He seems to have lacked stamina to endure the long strain they were all exposed to after I left for Ningbo; and as I was over a month absent, it was a testing time for them all, for the worst was over before I could return.

I am glad to say I have found nearly all the Christians have stood firm, only one having gone back. He seems to have lacked stamina to endure the long strain they were all exposed to

Others have got a new start, and are bolder in the faith than formerly, and some new converts have been drawn out; so on the whole I do not think we have lost much, and may be all the better for this searching.

It has been a time to bring out all that was in us, both natives and foreigners; but those who put their trust in God shall never be ashamed. Ever since the night of the riot, the Lord has been showering blessings on us and since the buildings began we have not been stopped an hour by rain. It has come now, but the roofs are on, and no harm or hindrance will result, which is a blessing."

We had, about that time, two hundred Christians and inquirers, and out of that number only two turned back through fear. The poor, scattered flock had met in little groups in each other's houses, the stronger visiting and cheering on the weaker and more timid.

Mr. Stott arrived on Friday and at once set a few men to clear away the debris and erect a few upright poles and cross-beams, over which were thrown bamboo mats; and by Saturday afternoon the extempore chapel was ready to receive the flock who came to welcome their pastor back.

And what a day of thanksgiving it was, both rejoicing together.

God was very gracious to us in this time of sore trial; the blow had been especially heavy, because unexpected. We had gone through so much in the earlier years, had lived down opposition and hatred and had gathered a goodly number of warm-hearted Christians. It seemed as if our difficulties were over and we had reached the reaping time; but with one stroke all our hopes appeared laid in the grave – yet, only appeared.

When I received the letter from my husband which told me everything we possessed was destroyed, and that he and the helpless band of eighteen natives were in Ningbo and had taken possession of a large empty house, homeless and almost clotheless, the blow seemed cruel; yet, at the same time, God brought His own Word to my comfort.

The blow seemed cruel; yet, at the same time, God brought His own Word to my comfort.

It was as though the question was asked afresh, "Why do the heathen rage and the people imagine a vain thing?"

That one word, *vain,* had a power I never felt before.

Thank God all should be vain, we should yet go back, gather our scattered people, build up our ruined home and chapels, and win many more souls for our Lord and Master.

The vision filled me with hope and comfort, and when, three hours afterwards, I left to join my husband, it was with a heart profoundly thankful, for had not the precious lives been spared, and was there not good hope for the future?

I thought God had comforted me, so that I might be able to speak words of cheer and comfort to the dear ones who had passed through the storm; but when we met next morning they had no need of my comfort – God had gone before and cheered them with His own assurance that all would yet be well and wonderfully did God fulfil His promise, for on the first Sunday at the opening of our new chapel, five persons were baptized and received into the church; and for years after, few months passed without some being added to our number.

Many men were employed, so that the school and chapel might be finished with as little delay as possible. Services were held each night for the workmen, but with that exception and our Sunday services, our missionary work was at a standstill.

One day, upon my remarking to Mr. Stott that he was building substantial walls, he replied, "I want to build this specially strong, for I believe Christ is coming very soon and the Jews are to be the evangelisers of the world, and when they come to Wenzhou, it is my desire they shall find a place ready for them."

"I want to build this specially strong, for I believe Christ is coming very soon and the Jews are to be the evangelisers of the world, and when they come to Wenzhou, it is my desire they shall find a place ready for them."

About a year after this, we had a letter from the Rev. David Hill, of Hankou, saying that he had just baptized a man who dated his first interest in the Gospel to the time of the riot. He had come to Wenzhou on business, and when he saw the missionary robbed of all he possessed, pelted with stones, making his way very quietly to the Yamen without one word of cursing or bitterness, such as he expected; and when, a few weeks later, that missionary returned quietly to rebuild, with as much grace as if all the city were his friends, he said to himself, the religion which could bring forth fruit like that was worth inquiring into.

On returning to his home, he attended Mr. Hill's chapel, and was in due time baptized by him: thus the Lord gave us fruit in the very midst of the fire.

But we were not allowed to go without personal suffering. We were living in a low, damp Chinese house and the wet season coming on, we were compelled to move into the new home before it was dry. Miss Little John, a young missionary, who had joined us but a few months, was taken seriously ill and died in the autumn of the same year at Yantai.

I take an extract from a letter written to a friend at this time,

September 14, 1885.

DEAR B,

Very many thanks for your cheering letter received two weeks ago. Just when it came we were getting weary and discouraged, and your sympathy cheered us not a little. It is not often we feel down-hearted, but I fear we are somewhat in that condition at present.

We are still left single-handed (Miss Little John being away invalided), and we begin to feel the strain heavier than we can bear.

We do not mind hard work, but it is discouraging to feel that, work as we will, one half is left undone.

I have now twenty-five girls entirely under my care, who need and ought to have all my time. The dear ones who were converted last year are growing in grace, and their thirst for the Word of God *must* be satisfied. On the other hand, the Christian women and inquirers need much teaching, and in trying to do both, neither is done thoroughly.

The same is true of my husband.

The church in this city has grown to need all his time and care, yet he is grieved that the out-stations are not visited oftener.

May our Father lead us in a right way. I am sure you will pray for us.

Let me now turn from the discouraging to the encouraging. I never like to look long at the dark side, it does not pay. We need all the hope and joy we can bring into this work, especially in such a dry and thirsty land.

Praise the Lord, we find Him a well-spring in the desert. He gives strength according to our day, filling our hands full of sheaves and causing our hearts to rejoice, so that we should not, if we could, change places with any one.

Month by month, some are coming out on the Lord's side. At Bing-yei, where Mrs. Liu has gone for a month, quite a number have put away their idols and are inquiring after the truth. Four young men at one hamlet, three women at another, and so on.

Mrs. Liu has gone to teach them. At the same place, one of our old Christians passed away lately. He was an old man and failing for some time. One day he felt unable to get up, and said to his wife that Jesus was coming for him soon. In the afternoon he asked for some food, and when he had taken a little, he said, 'Jesus is coming for me now, I will just sleep a little till He comes; don't wake me.'

He fell asleep and never opened his eyes on earth again. (This was the old man found worshipping in the temple by the schoolboy Z-nüe.)

At another station, Dong-ling, where there are about forty Christians, eight families have put away their idols and are asking after the truth. No doubt some of them are chosen of the Lord.

As soon as the weather gets a little cooler, my husband hopes to take on some young men students again, and I a few women, for training during the winter months. I can take in ten or twelve women to teach, without adding very much to my labour. They can share morning and evening Bible classes with the girls, and a class every afternoon for them would be all the extra work it would give me. We have also begun a boys' day school.

This was much needed for the sons of the Christians and there are ten pupils.

The Lord has given us more than we asked.

My husband and myself both suffered, and it was then seeds of the disease in Mr. Stott, which two years later compelled us to go to England, were sown, and afterwards developed into the painful complications which in the spring of 1889 ended in his translation to glory.

Thus we were called to be sufferers together with Christ in no ordinary way, yet no word of regret ever passed his lips. He was full of praise that God had enabled him to serve more than twenty years in China.

In the beginning of the year 1886, my husband felt much led to ask God to give him at least one soul each Sunday.

Week by week he kept this request before the Lord, pleading there might be no barren week during the year; and at its close we were much interested to find that just fifty-two persons had been added to our church.

I remember my husband looking into my face with a sad expression as he said, "Why did I not ask more? Oh, how we limit God, when He might do great things for us if only we would open our mouths wide unto Him!"

CHAPTER 9

WINNING THE LOST

"And ye shall be witnesses unto Me." Acts 1:8

It will be interesting to give a few instances of the kind of men and women whom God has chosen as instruments for the furtherance of His own work.

In 1880, Dr. Douthwaite had, for a time, a hospital in this city for the cure of opium-smokers, and amongst the degraded applicants was a silver-smith named Li Ao-ming.

This man was in the last stage of degradation and poverty. He had to borrow the dollars necessary to ensure his admittance into the refuge, and the only shirt he possessed was borrowed too. He had a bold, defiant, repulsive look, had been an opium-smoker for many years, and was such a desperately wicked character that his own mother did not like to own him.

After he had been in the refuge a few days he began to take an interest in the services held by the assistant, and slowly his mind opened up to receive the truth. Few knew what was going on in the man's mind until one day, when going upstairs to his room, another opium patient deliberately spilt the dirty water he was carrying down over Ao-ming's clothes!

Instead of flying into a passion and cursing the man, as he would have done a week or two before, he stepped down until the man descended; then looking him steadily in the face, said, " If you had done this to me a week ago, I would have cursed you, your parents, and your ancestors for generations; but I have heard of the love of Jesus, dying for such guilty men as we are, and I will not curse you again."

When the time came for him to leave, having got rid of that terrible opium habit, which is as a chain which closely binds its poor victims, he begged to be allowed to remain a fortnight longer, so that he might learn more of the precious truth.

As soon as he left the refuge, he went home to tell his mother and two brothers of the wonderful gospel which he had heard and believed, and which had changed his heart and made him hate the things he loved before. His mother and brothers were much interested and began to attend the services.

They lived in a part of the city where no work had begun and at my request, the mother opened her house for a meeting once a week. This was continued for over a year, so that the neighbours had the opportunity of hearing of a Saviour's love. The mother became a true Christian and, more than a year afterwards, fell asleep rejoicing in her Saviour.

His two brothers were baptized with him, but one of them has shown by his life that he was never saved, and was expelled from the church four years afterwards. The other brother still remains with us, but has never been much more than a dead-and-alive Christian.

Ao-ming very soon took up his trade again as a silversmith. Sometimes he would be two days in a village, sometimes a week, according to the amount of work he had to do, but every night after the day's work was over, and every Sunday wherever he happened to be, he spent in telling the glad Good News.

He was a wonder to himself, and as is often the case with such people, he was mostly taken up with telling what God had done for him. His earnest, fearless manner arrested attention, and it was not long before we had many inquirers asking for more teaching, saying the silversmith had first told them of a Saviour's love. His zeal sometimes went beyond his knowledge, and we had often to undo some of his work, but he was much used of God nevertheless.

After some years my husband, being in need of an evangelist, decided to try the silversmith. He worked both hard and earnestly, but he had an overbearing manner which spoilt much of his work, and after a time he was allowed to go back to his trade as being the best thing for a man of his disposition.

It was all the same whether he was a paid evangelist or a working silversmith, preach he would, and preach he did, and he was the means of the salvation of many souls. He has never been an easy man to guide; bold, hasty, and self-conceited. He has had to be kept in with a firm hand, but when his faults are firmly though kindly pointed out, he often confesses with bitter tears.

About five years ago he opened a shop in the village of Bahzie, about thirteen miles from here, and after settling his shop affairs, the next thing he did was to look out for a room in which he could preach on Sundays, the rent of which he paid himself. On the first Sunday morning he closed his shop, hanging a board outside which announced that no business could be transacted that day, and it was well known that the time was spent in preaching.

After a time, a number of inquirers gathered round him, and it became necessary to have a chapel. This matter he took up entirely himself, giving what he could and seeking help from the city Christians until he had received about seventy dollars.

With this money he mortgaged a small house, which he had repaired and put in order for a chapel, and since he has become the pastor of this little self-supporting church. But though doing a good work, the people sometimes get tired of him, for after all there is a great mixture of Christ and Ao-ming in all he says; still God has blessed and is blessing his labours, and we rejoice, though, if we had our way, he would be a different man.

Once a month we send a fresh preacher to help the few Christians. Ao-ming is now a prosperous tradesman, liberal and open-handed, very hospitable, and in spite of many faults we praise God for him.

On the anniversary of my twenty-five years' work in Wenzhou, he felt very proud to present me with a silk banner entirely on his own account, as a token of his love and esteem.

Then there is Boa-sang-tsang, former firewood seller. I cannot recall anything about this man's conversion.

He was baptized in 1877, about the time we left for England on our first furlough. By the time we returned at the end of 1878, he had already won several persons to Christ. He was very poor, carrying his firewood from door to door, but in whichever house he entered where he had opportunity he preached Christ to the inmates.

It was thus Mrs. Liu and others were won to Christ. Fearless and utterly careless of rebuke, it could be said literally that as he went he preached. After a few years of such soul-winning, he was sent out as an evangelist; faithfully and earnestly he worked, never weary, though often unwise.

Later on, my husband had, for a time, to suspend him from preaching, because he had taken needless offence at a trifle, and seemed to be doing more harm than good amongst the Christians.

He was spoken to very gently, but firmly, and helped back to his old trade again for a short time; but his repentance was truly beautiful, and when in 1887 we left on our second furlough, it was very touching to see Mr. Boa, though suspended as a preacher, following my husband's chair weeping like a child, proving that "faithful are the wounds of a friend."

The year after he was made a colporteur, and ever since has been doing noble work in that line. He has been the means of opening up many new districts, one of which, O-dzing, had very soon afterwards to go through the baptism of fire.

O-dzing is a small village situated amongst the hills, about fourteen miles from Wenzhou. The first believers were a mother and two sons of a well-to-do family.

Mr. Boa remained two or three weeks instructing them in the truth, and quite a number in the village began to show interest. The head-man of the district, feeling annoyed at the desertion from the ranks of those who supported the idols, determined, if possible, to intimidate the believers.

After Mr. Boa left, a younger and more inexperienced preacher was sent, and while he was there persecution began. The preacher was beaten, and the Christian and her son tied up by the thumbs until she should recant. An attack was then made upon their house, the inmates had to escape out of doors or windows any way they could, while everything within was either smashed or stolen.

The granaries were opened and the grain carried away. The family fled to Wenzhou, and the matter had to be put into the Consul's hands, and it was over a year before a settlement could be arrived at. Both sides suffered heavily. The Christians, who had lost over two hundred dollars, were only compensated to the extent of fifty-two dollars. While it cost their enemies three hundred dollars to get the case out of the Yamen. This has left a bitter feeling which has never been entirely uprooted, and the Gospel has been much hindered in that place through it.

It is remarkable that in every case where a lawsuit has been necessary, hindrance to the Gospel has been the result. We have always found it better for both Christians and heathen to settle disputes in a friendly way out of court. This becomes increasingly easy as the heathen gain confidence in the just judgment of the missionary. When they find that he does not take the part of the Christian because he is a Christian, they are willing to submit the case to him and abide by his decision. This is the last case of persecution which I have had to deal with through the Consul and I trust it will long remain the last. We have had many troubles since, but I have never failed in a friendly settlement.

Another interesting case was that of a husband and wife who had formerly been beggars. They had one little girl, whom they betrothed to a little orphan boy, who had a small house and an acre or two of ground. Yaih-zing-pah and his wife worked this little bit of ground diligently, which, however, only supported them part of the year; for the rest they had to beg.

Wandering into the chapel one day, he heard the Gospel preached, believed the truth, and was baptized in 1883. As soon as the little boy's relations knew, they insisted he must either give up this new doctrine or their relative. Everything was done to induce them to change their decision, but in vain. Yaih-zing-pah told them he could not give up Christ, who had done so much for him, saving his soul and giving heavenly riches which were beyond all this world could bestow. There was nothing for it but to turn out again into the cold world as homeless beggars.

Mr. Stott advised him to get work if possible, and for this purpose gave him a little money to erect a hut on an uncultivated hill, which he was allowed to work for a merely nominal rent.

Surely never were twenty dollars more usefully invested. Ten dollars were spent on building a house and ten dollars upon farming implements. The good couple set to work with a will. They asked if their house might be used for services on Sunday, so that those living near might hear the Gospel.

One day, a young man came to their door begging. He was the victim of the dreadful opium habit, of a respectable family, and could read well, but cast out from his home. He had no resource but begging from those nearly as poor as himself. Our friends told this young man of the God they worshipped, who was able to help him to break off the opium. They invited him to stay with them, promising to give him his food if he would work.

In the meantime they taught, helped, and prayed with him until the desire for opium was overcome, and he felt himself a free man once more. This poor fellow, the fruit of their labours, has been an earnest, consistent Christian for the last ten years, and is now an unpaid local preacher.

He continued working with them as a son, and three years ago was married to a deaf-and-dumb girl (he was too poor to pay for any other), and a year after she was received into the church. She is in all things consistent, but we can never know how she received the truths of the Gospel.

Yaih-zing-pah and his wife were also the means indirectly of opening up Tung-tso work. A beggar family called, who were friends in their old begging days, and were as usual invited to stay a few days and hear of Christ. After their begging tour of a few months they returned to their home in Tung-tso, and began to tell their neighbours of the new doctrine they had heard, but did not believe.

This created interest, so that when Mr. Boa some time afterwards on a book-selling tour visited the place, he found quite a number of people desiring to be taught. Upon his report we sent a preacher, and thus the work was begun in a district which heretofore the Truth had never entered, and we have now a little church with out-stations.

These beggars never believed the Truth for themselves, though they were the means of stirring up interest in others. Amongst the believers in that place were four young lads, very bright and earnest. These we brought into Wenzhou for two years' Bible training; two are now unpaid local preachers in their own district, while earning their living as farmers, and two are learning useful trades in the city and teach in Sunday school.

These beggars never believed the Truth for themselves, though they were the means of stirring up interest in others.

A few months ago, Yaih-sing~pah's wife was crossing the river in a boat with twenty others, when on her way to the chapel a strong wind capsized the boat, and our dear sister and sixteen others were drowned.

We mourn her. They had lost their daughter who was a bright little Christian some years ago, and now the old man is left alone in his sorrow.

Another worker is Mr. Dzing, who was brought to us when quite a little lad. His mother was dead, and his father a wretched opium-smoker, who had sold his younger brother for a few dollars to a man who took him off in a Fujian ship.

He was about to sell this little fellow, when a relative rescued and brought him to our school. He was a nervous boy, and for months Mr. Stott was pained to see him timidly shrink from him; but love and kindness won its way, and he became quite confiding.

His father left the district and troubled no more about his child, who was thus left absolutely in our hands. He was a quiet, studious lad, and it was seldom we had to find fault with his conduct. He was good and obedient, and outwardly all we could desire, but several years passed before the truth took possession of his heart.

When he was old enough he wanted to learn foreign printing, and our mission press being in Zhenjiang, we sent him there in the hope he would learn that trade. The reports we had of his conduct were satisfactory, but there was no one to teach printing, and as far as learning the trade was concerned it was a failure.

He had the advantage, however, of going to several places, visiting Japan amongst the others, so that he returned to us quite a travelled Chinaman. About 1878 he was converted and began to take part in preaching, and after a while he was employed as an evangelist and did good work, until in an hour of temptation he fell into sin, and had not only to be dismissed from preaching, but suspended from the church.

His repentance proving sincere, he was restored and three years after again became a preacher, and has ever since been a faithful, earnest, and most helpful worker. He is now pastor of the Bing-yie church. It was formerly an out-station from Wenzhou, but is now itself a centre, having out-stations of its own.

One of our disappointments in connection with the young man was his marrying a heathen girl in preference to a Christian, because the latter have large or natural feet. The disgrace of a wife with these seemed more than he could bear, when there were but few such, and each one had to bear reproach.

Now it is different. Not only have our girls increased in numbers, but many of our Christian women have unbound their feet, and are no longer the laughing stock of their neighbours. Mr. Dzing did not suffer from this false step so severely as some have had to do. His wife was a quiet, nice girl, and after some years was converted, but she has never been much help to him, either in the home or in spiritual life, through the lack of early training.

Another of our old boys is Mr. Tsiu; he was the first lad brought to Mr. Stott when he began his school in 1868. A more hopeless-looking, blank-faced boy you could hardly meet, and had it not been for the necessity of making a beginning with any kind of material that was brought to one's hand, he might never have been received.

His father was dead; his mother was a hard-hearted woman from the Fujian border, who had drowned two of her girls, kept a low-class inn, and was utterly without principle. His elder brother was a wretched opium-smoker. This boy had been born paralysed down one side, and it was because he could neither work nor walk properly, and was therefore only a burden, that he was brought to the foreigner.

Mr. Stott's faith in the power of God was great, and he trusted that even this unpromising lad might yet be a useful witness for Christ, and he was not disappointed.

He learned quickly and became a good scholar. He had been in the school about four years, and understood well the plan of salvation, though he had not accepted it. Our old Ningbo woman induced him to read the Scriptures to her every night, and on one occasion she said to him, "How is it you can read so beautifully and yet. don't believe?"

He replied, "I am not good enough."

"Oh… " she answered, "you are like the man who went into the feast without the wedding garment. You don't want Christ's robe, but are trying to make your own do."

A few nights after he dreamed a strange dream: he thought he heard the trumpet announce the Lord's coming; that in terror he got up, dressed, and went out to meet Him. When he got into the courtyard he thought he saw Mr. Stott going out of the gate. He called upon him to wait but Mr. Stott answered, "No, the Lord has come: I must go out to meet Him; you are not saved, you must be left behind."

In terror he awoke, and was glad to find it only a dream! But the next day, on telling his strange story to one of the Christians, the question was brought home, "What if it had been true?" He saw his danger, and at once yielded his heart to the Lord, and we have never had cause to doubt the reality of his conversion, though some weak points have often given us sorrow. He became an eloquent effective preacher, and was for several years my husband's right hand.

CHAPTER 10

THE FRUIT

"How beautiful are the feet of them that preach the gospel of peace, and bring glad tidings of good things!" Romans 10:15

Z-nüe was another of our schoolboys who was much owned of God. He was brought to us when about eleven years of age. I well remember seeing a little bright-faced lad led in, clad in a rather nice though worn silk garment.

I was surprised to see a boy of such well-to-do appearance, for surely, thought I, the father who could clothe his son in silk, could afford to give him rice. For up to this point no one had come to the school for the sake of the education and training. In every case they were too poor to give them food.

Now here is an exception, thought I, the first of a superior set of boys. But alas! The next morning the father came with a profuse apology - the silk garment had been borrowed, and must be returned to its owner; and when it was taken off, oh what rags, and dirty rags too.

I had at once to have new clothes made for the little fellow, and the old ones burnt.

From the first he took a liking for us; there was nothing of the shyness and fear that most exhibited for a few days. Some of the other boys would laugh at him when he came up with a bright smile, perfectly fearless, to share with me some of the beans and nuts, or anything else that had been given to him, and when he could get a flower to present me with he was highly delighted.

Slowly the truth began to take possession of his young mind. With him there was no sudden conversion, but rather a gradual taking in and understanding of the truth; but the change in his life was no less decided, and when he was fourteen years of age, there being no doubt in our minds as to the reality of his conversion, he was baptized and received into church fellowship.

He continued his studies for a few years longer, and it was in the meantime, while still considered a schoolboy, that he went to Bing-yie, and was the means of the conversion of the old man, worshipping in the temple.

For fourteen years afterwards he was a consistent, godly, and earnest Christian, and for nearly ten years of that time a faithful preacher. He contracted a disease of the lungs, and in spite of every effort to save so valuable a life, God took him when he was about twenty-eight years of age. Eternity alone will reveal how many he was the means of leading to Christ, for winning souls was almost a passion with him.

When he was about twenty-five years of age, his parents, without his knowledge or consent, betrothed him to a young girl of fourteen, and at this we were greatly grieved, for we had hoped he would have married a Christian from the school, and thus be helped in his work.

However, engagements entered into by parents are not to be set aside, and there was nothing for it but to try and get the girl into the school, and to seek by God's blessing to win her to Christ. The parents on both sides being willing she was brought, under a written agreement, to remain with us for five years; when she arrived from the country she was taken first of all to her future husband's home, and introduced to the family as their daughter, and by them brought to us.

She was a very pretty girl, bright and more obedient than most were when first they came to us. We were therefore the more surprised when three or four days afterwards she disappeared.

We searched everywhere, sent to the young man's home, but no trace of her could be found.

A messenger was sent to her own home, where she was found quietly doing household work. She had run off, asked her way to the north gate, took her passage in a boat without any money to pay it, and arrived at her mother's house after six hours' journey.

It was the most plucky thing I had ever known a Chinese girl to do, and when she returned with the messenger I decided to take very little notice of the escapade, thinking that fear of the foreigner was the cause; but when about a week after that she was caught in the act of running away a second time, we decided to take some action.

I put her in a room and told her that, not having time to speak to her now, I must lock the door, as she was not to be trusted. It was more than an hour afterwards before I could return.

I asked her to tell me plainly what her difficulty was; why did she run away?

No answer.

Was she afraid of me? I asked.

She said "No."

Were the other girls unkind to her?

She answered "No."

Why then had she run away, for no one had ever done so before?

For a time she was silent, but I encouraged her to speak, promising, if it was anything I could remove, it should be done. She then opened up her heart quite freely. She said she had been engaged contrary to her own wish, and when she was brought to the young man's home, and saw how very poor they were, and that even their language she did not understand (they were Tai-chow people), she determined she would not marry him.

But, I said, you don't know the young man himself, you have never seen him; if you did, perhaps you would change your mind.

But she answered, "No; I would like to stay here, and if you will promise me I need not marry into that family I shall stay and do all you tell me."

I pointed out how impossible it was for me to give such a promise, that the engagement contracted by parents on both sides was binding; "but," I said, "I can promise one thing, that if you will wait quietly for three years, during which time you will have opportunities of seeing the young man. If, then, after knowing him better, you are still of the same mind, still unwilling to marry him, I will use my influence with him, and I have little doubt but that he will release you."

At that her face brightened; she said, " If you will promise me that, it will be alright; you need not lock the door, for I shall not try to run away again."

And from that time she scarcely ever gave me an anxious thought, being both obedient and affectionate, learned quickly, and became a true Christian. Before the three years were over, the young man's mother died, and she of her own accord put on mourning for her, thus showing that she had accepted him.

When we left for England in 1887, Z-nüe was evidently dying of consumption, and we, fearing his father might sell her to some other man, obtained, with the girl's consent, a document from him handing the girl over to us. We on our part promising to return the betrothal money paid by his father; so that after his death she was perfectly free.

She was later on married to a Christian young man.

Another interesting case was that of Ling-ah-chang, who lived outside the east gate.

He was an iron-beater by trade. I cannot now recall the incidents of his conversion, but he became a very earnest, useful Christian.

He started a meeting in his mother's house, so that the neighbours around might hear of Christ, and became quite eloquent in preaching. His mother and brother were converted through his instrumentality. After two or three years he became a useful local preacher.

In 1888, when we were in England, Mr. G. engaged him first as an evangelist and afterwards as pastor of a small church, and from that time he has been doing good and earnest work.

His dear old mother died last year, a most triumphant death, rejoicing in the prospect of being with Christ, which she realised was "far better." He married one of the girls from the school, and she has been a great help in work amongst the women.

Mr. Tsie was a native of the Dong-ling district, where he worked at his trade, that of a shoemaker. About seventeen years ago, when twenty-two years of age, he first heard of the "foreign doctrine" through a Christian relative of his who lived nearby. This Christian at last persuaded him to attend the Sunday services held at our chapel ten miles off.

Mr. Stott went there once a month to instruct the converts, and, assisted by good native preachers, faithfully told out the Gospel story. The young man attended pretty regularly for about two months, but understood very little. Nothing of the precious truth seemed to enter his heart or find any lodgment there. He would sneer to himself as the believers sung the hymns which sounded so outlandish to him, and would say to himself, "Well, those are barbarian sounds. TThose who believe this foreign gospel will turn rebels soon, and we shall have a rebellion in the country." After that, he relapsed into his old ways and absolutely refused to accompany his relative to the services. Some months passed, when, without any apparent preparation or cause, a great change came.

One day he was sitting outside his door mending shoes. In front was a large tree and, as he looked at it, he began to consider the trunk, branches, and leaves. There they were, sure enough, but where did they come from? There must be a root, even though unseen by him. Then it flashed across his mind that that was just like the world. Here was he; here were his neighbours and friends, and before them their fathers and grandfathers and more distant ancestors; but, surely, to all, there must be a root - some great ancestor above them all. There and then he realised the truth that there is a God from whom we - everyone - have our being.

From that day forward all was changed. When he awakened in the morning he felt like a new man, and forthwith, ignorant as he was, he began preaching the great Truth that had taken possession of his heart.

It was some months after this change before he got assurance that his sins were all forgiven; but he dates his conversion from that day, when, as it were, God commanded the tree to preach a parable to him. He understood little of the plan of salvation, and could not read a character in the Bible, but he spoke out what he knew. He told of the one true God - of how He has given us all good things we possess, and yet we daily sin against Him; and how we all were deserving of hell fire, but that God would hear us when we pray to Him, and if we trust Him fully He would save.

He understood little of the plan of salvation, and could not read a character in the Bible, but he spoke out what he knew. He told of the one true God.

On and on he preached in this strain as long as any would stop to listen, and afterwards he said it was one of the strangest things to him that, when able to read the Bible for himself, he found it tallied exactly with many things he said in those old days, thus showing that the Spirit in the Word and the Spirit in the heart is one.

His old relative was delighted, and soon after the preachers and other Christians, who heard of his changed life and earnestness, sought to teach him more clearly about the things of God. It was not long 'ere all the Christians in his village suffered severe persecution, but though he had never heard that the Scriptures exhorted to endure persecution joyfully, still he and all did indeed rejoice to suffer for Christ, and in the midst of the fire sang hymns, prayed, and praised that they were counted worthy to suffer for His dear name's sake.

In after days he often expressed the wish that he had now the same deep earnestness and longing to lead others to the light which he had in the beginning of his Christian life.

Wherever he went - walking on the roads, in boats, inns, or in houses - he told the story. To him it was so wonderful, he thought he had only to tell others and they too would believe.

Later on, Mr. Stott, hearing what a promising young preacher he seemed to be, invited him to the Mission House in Wenzhou, to study. He made very rapid progress both in his Christian life and studies. Since then he has been an earnest and true Bible student. For a few years he continued at his trade, but at the same time doing all in his power to help forward the work, and took regular services in his native village.

In course of time he married one of our Christian schoolgirls, who has been a true helpmeet to him, helping in the work amongst women and children, besides keeping her home in such cleanly comfort as is seldom seen in China.

In 1887, when the out-stations of Bing-yie and Dong-ling were given over to two young missionaries to be henceforth worked as separate stations, Mr. Stott handed over to them Mr. Dzang and Mr. Tsie as two of our most efficient helpers. For years he did valuable work there, until about four years ago, when he came to help me at Wenzhou. He has been my right hand and greatest comfort since, for though others have done good and valuable work, he, by his deeply spiritual character and knowledge of the Word of God, has been a most valued teacher, as well as pastor of our large Wenzhou church.

Sa-loe-sz-mo, our Bible-woman, has a bright round face which beams upon you at all times. I have often wondered, in looking into that face, whether her sad life's history, which she had often told, could indeed be true.

Not only has the past been full of sadness, but even now there is nothing in her home surroundings which can account for her cheery, happy smile. Truly God has given her His own peace and joy, which the world can neither give nor take away. She was only a little child when she was betrothed to a man twenty years her senior, and taken to her future husband's home to be henceforth completely under the rule of her mother-in-law, who seems to have been a hard, unkind woman.

The child was both hot-headed and warm-hearted. A little love would have brought out her better qualities, but with hard words and harder treatment she grew reckless and disobedient, ever ready to answer back if found fault with. Of course this only made her mother-in-law more unkind and bitter. It was most pathetic to hear our little woman tell of how desperate she used to get, and how, after being scolded and beaten, she longed to put an end to her miserable existence.

Sometimes she even went so far as to try to strangle herself; but, feeling the choking sensation, would get frightened· and let herself go in time. How wonderful was God's goodness in restraining her. She little knew then that she was His chosen vessel to bring cheer, gladness, and life to many a heart as sad as her own; for, alas! Hers was no uncommon case - only a specimen of the many, many little daughters-in-law living a life of slavery, receiving as reward scoldings and blows.

About ten years ago, not very long after her marriage, a young neighbour-woman became interested in the Gospel. Soon this woman was converted and became earnest in telling others the Good News. After her conversion she was visited by Christians and preachers, who were ever glad of an opening to tell of Christ's love to those neighbours whom she had gathered and whom she was anxious to interest in her new-found treasure. After the first curiosity was appeased, very few cared to listen and only into one heart prepared by the Holy Spirit did the seed seem to fall and take root, and that heart was Sa-loe-sz-mo's.

Impelled by some, as yet, unknown power, she would go whenever possible, either to hear her neighbour's visitors, or to talk over the strange new things with her friend privately. As soon as her husband and mother-in-law found she was truly interested in what they called the "foreign doctrine" they tried to prevent her going out, complained of her wasting time, and forbade her to listen any more.

Her only chance, then, was to steal out in the evening, when her day's work was done, to her friend's house, and there talk quietly, ask questions, and learn to pray.

For many months things went on thus, but as she became more and more interested she longed for more spiritual food and begged to be allowed to go to the chapel on Sundays. The very mention of this desire brought down upon her a storm of petty persecution; but by that time she was slowly learning to restrain her tongue, and instead of answering back, as formerly, would retire to pray and to ask the Lord to open up a way for her.

She tried very hard every day to be specially good towards her ill-tempered mother-in-law and to do more than her usual amount of silk spinning. By Saturday evening she had succeeded so well, that when she asked, with fear and trembling, to be allowed to go to chapel next day, she was surprised by a favourable reply; and thus, by result of great effort and industry, the little woman used to get permission to accompany her friend to the Sunday services, and it was not long before she was truly converted.

After that she had to endure bitter persecution.

Her husband often beat and ill-used her for believing "the doctrine," but her manifest change of behaviour, her industry, patience, and brightness at last conquered the prejudices of both mother and husband.

Not long ago, when some of the neighbours laughed at him for his weakness in allowing his wife to leave the worship of their forefathers, he answered, "A religion that is able to change and make her a much better wife mμst be good, and I shall not be the one to hinder."

The mother-in-law is now dead, and the husband, though unconverted, allows her to do as she pleases. She has been an earnest, active Bible-woman for four years, and has been the means of leading many of her dark sisters into the light of God's love. She has unbound her feet - which means a good deal to a Chinese woman - so that she may be better fitted for country work. She often has to walk ten or fifteen miles in the day. Often when we have been out together, I have retired quite worn out with the day's labours, while she, who had done so much or more than I, would continue till midnight teaching the Christians and inquirers.

During the two hottest months, when it is impossible to go out much, she refuses her salary, preferring to support herself by tea-picking, silk-weaving, or otherwise. She is only thirty years of age, and thus rather young, according to Chinese etiquette, to go about alone, and when not accompanied by myself or one of the young ladies, I always send an elderly woman with her; but her conduct is so wise and discreet that no one has ever hinted that her youth was any barrier to her usefulness.

Her cheery helpfulness makes her a favourite with the women, while her sturdy independence calls forth the respect of all. Her words carry conviction, so that even rough country men are compelled to listen to her quietly and respectfully. Her loving sympathy opens up the hearts of the people, and prepares the way for any straightforward words she may have to say about things which are not right in the lives of any of the Christians.

She is not afraid to speak out, though doing it in such a manner as rarely produces any bad feeling. We look upon her as a God-sent gift to the Church.

One of our most devoted and intelligent women is Ling-di-na, who had formerly been a great opium-smoker. She was now a widow, but she had begun that pernicious habit while her husband was alive, he too being a victim of the drug. She was a silk-weaver, and the constant sitting over her work, together with poor food, brought on a painful internal trouble, for which she sought relief in opium, and thus the habit was formed.

Soon work, home duties, and everything good and true was given up, and she lived only to smoke and enjoy the soothing after-effects; as she herself said, "all pride and self-respect were lost." The confirmed opium-smoker will not work if he can get the drug without, and, when reduced to poverty, will pawn or sell everything he possesses, even wife, child-all must go to procure that which has become to him more than life.

By and by her husband died, and some time later a friend, by no means a bright Christian, persuaded her to accompany her to hear the Gospel. She attended regularly, when one day her only son was taken ill and died. In her grief she refused to be comforted, and would not go near the chapel. The Christians, however, did not forsake her. They held a little service over the child, and tried to persuade her to stay in our compound and break off the opium. She half promised, and that night knelt down to pray for the first time. She told God what they wanted her to do, but that now her baby was gone, she did not care what became of her. If only she could see her child again she would be comforted. They had told her it was in heaven with Jesus, and that, if she believed, she would go there and see it by and by. If that were true, and the Lord would give her some evidence that her child was indeed living, she would go the next day to get the opium medicine and become a true "Jesus disciple."

She went to bed, and that night was granted to her a wonderful vision - the room was flooded with light, and scene after scene was presented to her. I cannot recall all she said, but in one scene she saw our two young ladies dressed in white. "Ah, they are in heaven" she thought; "but my baby is not there."

Again, she saw a beautiful boy: "That must be the Lord Jesus when at twelve years of age he was lost in Jerusalem." Then she saw a beautiful golden city, so bright and glorious that she knew at once it must be heaven; but still her child was nowhere to be seen.

At last she recognised him sitting on the golden pavement, as he had often sat on her mud floor, and her heart bounded with a great joy: "Yes, he surely was there, and she would believe, so that by and by she might meet him again."

The next morning saw her early at the China Inland Mission premises, asking medicine to break off the degrading habit, though she knew it meant much suffering.

This was eight years ago, and her Christian life has been without a shadow. When we were without a doctor, and Miss Bardsley was doing what she could to relieve some of the suffering around, this dear woman voluntarily gave up two mornings a week to preach to the women who came for treatment. In this and other ways she has been ever willing to do what she could for the spread of the gospel. She is well fitted for the work of Bible-woman, but physical weakness prevents her doing much country work, though she is always willing to accompany one or other of our young ladies when visiting nearer places.

CHAPTER 11

THE BORDERLAND BETWEEN LIFE AND DEATH

"When thou passest through the waters I will be with thee; and through the rivers, they shall not overflow thee." Isaiah 43:2

In 1886 we were joined by three new workers, Miss Oliver, who arrived in May, Mr. Grierson in June, and Mr. Sayers in July.

My husband and I had both felt that the work had grown too heavy for our shoulders. I wanted someone to relieve me of the girls' school, and he wanted young men to do more of the country work. In the autumn of that year, Mr. Stott handed over the two churches of Dong-ling and Bing-yie to the charge of the two young brethren. They were to live at Bing-yie and work in the surrounding districts, so what was an out-station before, became a new centre, from which stations were opened, these ever since having been a separate work. Mr. Sayers, after a few months, left for Chaozhou, where he was privileged to labour only a few months, for he was "called home" in the autumn of 1888. Mr. G. still continues in the charge of the Bing-yie work.

In 1887 we felt it necessary to take a change to England, Mr. Stott being considerably run down in health. Mr. Stott's health began to fail almost as soon as we left China, and by the time we reached England he was very ill; congestion of the lungs, combined with weak action of the heart, caused such difficulty of breathing that to lie down was impossible.

Night and day he sat in patient suffering for a year and eight months, although for most of that time he was able to go about and enjoy nature in all her lovely forms.

After three months spent with dear friends in London, we went to Dartmouth, and remained the winter and spring of 1887 and 1888 with the Misses Teage; there he was surrounded with every comfort that love and kindness could devise.

He had a donkey-carriage and drove himself for miles round the lovely country, while I walked and talked by his side. That winter was a memory he loved to dwell upon, the dear friends making a deep impression upon his heart.

Being in Scotland in the summer of 1888, we were invited to join Drs. Gordon and Pierson in a missionary tour, and as an eminent physician encouraged us with his opinion that frequent change of scene would benefit the dear invalid, we accompanied them. We had most remarkable blessing during the six weeks in which we visited all the principal cities and towns in the north. Large numbers, attracted by the eloquence of Drs. Gordon and Pierson, left deeply impressed by the wonderful story of what God had done among the heathen.

Mrs. Gordon and I conducted ladies' meetings in each place, I frequently speaking in the evening meetings as well; but while it was my privilege to engage in this more public work in my husband's stead, helped by his encouragement, sympathy, and prayers, he was doing a no less blessed work, for, though unable to attend any of the meetings, the holy, sweet influence of his life was telling most powerfully on those around him.

Everywhere our kind entertainers were deeply impressed with his not only patient but cheerful suffering, and many were won by him then who have been my warm friends ever since.

At the end of this tour the doctor said Mr. Stott was decidedly better, and if he would spend the winter in the south of France he might yet recover. So, in November, we left for Cannes, where we spent several months in a bright sunny home for invalids; but, in spite of care and doctors' skill, the disease gained upon him until, on April 21, 1889, Easter Sunday, he most triumphantly entered into the presence of his Lord.

As he was evidently, though slowly, growing weaker, I asked the doctor if the place were suitable, or if a change of climate would be of any use. He answered he would like a consultation before giving me an answer, for if it was as he feared no change would be of any use. After the consultation, my husband, looking the doctor full in the face, said, "Do you think I shall be able to return to China?"

The doctor, not wishing to tell the sad truth, turned the question aside. Mr. Stott, seeing the evasion, said, "Don't be afraid to tell me the worst, for there is no worst for me, thank God. I have had twenty years' service for Him in China; I did wish to go back, but if He says no, why should I desire it? I am willing to stay and suffer if it is His will; willing to go to China if it be His will." And then with a bright smile he added, "Why, I believe I am willing to go half-way to China and then go to heaven, if that were His will."

"Don't be afraid to tell me the worst, for there is no worst for me, thank God. I have had twenty years' service for Him in China; I did wish to go back, but if He says no, why should I desire it? I am willing to stay and suffer if it is His will;

The doctor looked at him earnestly and said, “I envy you.” He then told him plainly there was no hope of recovery. Not a shadow crossed the face. He knew where his home was and longed to go. I was not unprepared. I saw the daily weakening of the poor body and feared there could be no return of strength; but it was more difficult for me to submit to God’s will.

To him, God’s will had ever been first and he had no hard lesson to learn.

I remember a lady, who was strongly impressed with faith-healing views, talking with him during his first few months of illness. She said it was only a matter of faith; he might be better if he would; it was so easy just to have faith in God, and it would be done.

She asked, “Don’t you think God could heal you and send you back to your loved work?”

He replied, “My difficulty does not lie there; I know He could; but God once gave the desire of the heart and sent leanness to the soul. I do not want that. He knows if He gave me strength it will be used for His service, and if weakness, it will be borne for Him. I want Him to have His own way with me all through.”

God knows if He gave me strength it will be used for His service, and if weakness, it will be borne for Him. I want Him to have His own way with me all through.

The lady had nothing to answer; I think she must have felt as I did, that it was better to lie passively in God's hands than to refuse to suffer.

But I did not learn the lesson so quickly.

For a long time I wrestled and struggled for his life. For a while I hid from him my distress; but one night, unable to bear any longer, I sobbed out that I not let him go.

Calmly and quietly he said, “Not yet, dearie, not yet. God will make you willing when the time comes."

Three days after, God caused me to triumph in Christ. My will was swallowed up in His will, and all was peace. That evening, kneeling by his side, I was for the first time able to ask God to take him home, gently, quietly, and painlessly, and to take him soon.

While I was praying he gave a sigh of relief and said, "Thank God." When I had finished praying he said, "You don't know how much good these words have done me. I knew God would bring you to that point before He called me away. I was only waiting to hear you say such words as these. I have nothing more to desire - all is well."

For six weeks after this we lived together on the borderland.

Not for one moment did I ever wish to keep him back. We talked and prayed much, and almost went into heaven together. We made my plans for the future, even to the month in which I should start for China.

All had been talked over, and I was able to carry out the arrangements made by him even to the letter. It was a great joy to him to know that I was going back to take up his work, and to be both father and mother to the people he loved so dearly, for we had been as one in the work.

When I asked if he had any instructions for me, he said, "No, you know the people and work as well as I, and will do just as I have done. I have no care about that. Only give the native Christians my love, and tell them I would have returned to them if I could, but I shall wait for them, and by and by we shall meet."

CHAPTER 12

CROSSING THE JORDAN

The very wonderful way in which he realised the Lord's presence is related in a small pamphlet entitled, "*In Memoriam: George Stott,*" published by Morgan and Scott.

From this I quote the following letters, written to our C.I.M. secretary,

MAISON BLANCHE,

ROUTE DE GRASSE, CANNES,

April 23, 1889.

DEAR MR. BROOMHALL,

It was my privilege to be with our dear departed brother, Mr. Stott, during his last night on earth, and a few particulars of the closing scene will, I know, be acceptable to you.

Slowly, during many weeks of pain, the earthly house of this tabernacle was being dissolved, and on Saturday evening, about 9.30, one of the sisters came over to say that his sufferings had become more intense, and the end seemed approaching.

I was in the act of reading in the Christian classics, 'De Incarnation Verbi Dei,' the account by Athanasius of the triumphs of the early Christians and martyrs over death, due to their Lord and Master, who, by His Cross and Resurrection had vanquished death, so that they no longer feared but despised it.

"For," says he, "as when the sun rises after the night has passed, and the whole globe is illuminated by it, it is not at all doubtful that it is the sun which has shed its light everywhere, and has driven away the darkness and enlightened all things; so death being utterly despised and trampled down from the time when the Saviour's saving appearance in the body, and end upon the Cross took place, it is perfectly clear that it is the Saviour Himself, who appeared in the body, who brought death to naught, and daily exhibits trophies against it in His own disciples.

For when one sees men, who are by nature weak, leaping forth to death and not cowering before its corruption, nor displaying fear at the descent into Hades, but with zealous soul provoking it; and not shrinking from tortures, but for Christ's sake preferring rather than this present life to rush upon death; or, too, if one be a beholder of men and women and young children rushing upon and leaping forth to death for the religion of Christ; who is so simple, or who is so unbelieving, or is so incapacitated in mind, as not to perceive and draw the conclusion that Christ, to whom the men bear witness, Himself bestows and gives to each the victory over death, rendering it utterly weak in each of those who hold His faith and bear the sign of the Cross?

It was thus, I thought, sixteen hundred years ago, but how many times, in common with all Christian workers in this land, I have heard the popular dictum, *Le Christianisme a fait son temps,* "Christianity has had its day," "It is used out." And as I went forth to witness for the first time a death-bed scene, this thought was uppermost, "Will it ratify the affirmation of Athanasius, and show that after sixteen centuries the virtue of the Cross and Resurrection is in no degree diminished?"

Entering the chamber, I saw our dear brother sitting up in the armchair, supported by his dear wife and one of the nursing sisters. It was one of the distressing features of his illness that he was unable to lie down, and all these weary weeks of pain had been passed sitting, with no possibility of supporting the poor head or giving the body relief, only by occasionally leaning forward.

The strong man was bowed, and poor nature was in a pitiable plight. The props of the tent were being taken away, and the suppressed groans of the sufferer told of the silver cord being loosed, and the links being broken which bound the spirit to the earthly tenement.

When he knew I was present he expressed a decided wish that I should stay with him, which I was only too glad to do. As I look back on that night, I feel that not for any consideration would I have missed that scene of suffering and holy triumph.

Never before did I know how truly death is a vanquished enemy, its empire overthrown and its sceptre destroyed.

During eight hours we witnessed the King of Terrors doing his worst. The combat was a fierce one, blow after blow was dealt, strong pains were tearing at the vitals; the anguish of dissolution was there, but not for one moment did the spirit falter. With every moment's respite from pain he collected his little strength to give forth some word of testimony that the Lord was near, and doubt and fear far away. "It is only the poor body that is suffering," he said; "the soul is happy." Early in the evening he said, "I bless God that thirty years ago He washed me from my sins in His precious blood, and now the sun is shining without a cloud"; and thus with unfaltering faith, and with unwavering hope, he went down into the valley of the shadow.

Before leaving my house it came to my mind to glance at the portion for the evening in 'Daily Light,' and there indeed was a highway "cast up." Beautiful and appropriate it was, beginning with the words, "It is I; be not afraid. When thou passeth through the waters I will be with thee; and through the rivers they shall not overflow thee; when thou walkest through the fire thou shalt not be burned; neither shall the flame kindle upon thee: for I am the Lord thy God, thy Saviour. Though I walk through the valley of the shadow of death I will fear no evil: for Thou art with me; Thy rod and Thy staff they comfort me. Who shall separate us from the love of Christ? Shall tribulation, or distress, or persecution, or famine, or nakedness, or peril, or sword?"

I took it with me, that dear Mr. Stott might have a word like apples of gold in pictures of silver. In this 'royal road' we saw him advance, treading down with triumphant faith the powers of sin, and death, and hell.

The words he repeated the most were, "Come Lord Jesus, come now, come now," often reaching out his arms to welcome the Lord, whom he felt was indeed drawing near.

The words Mr. Stott repeated the most were, "Come Lord Jesus, come now, come now," often reaching out his arms to welcome the Lord, whom he felt was indeed drawing near.

Once or twice, in moments of extreme pain, his cry went up, "O Lord, help me; Lord, have mercy upon me."

The Lord heard him in the day of his distress, and strengthened him in the dire conflict. We sought to supply stones for his steps, as he forded the dark stream; words of life came spontaneously to our lips, and it was grand to see how his faith appropriated them.

When his dear wife reminded him that he would soon hear the Master's "Well done, good and faithful servant, enter thou into the joy of thy Lord," his soul seemed to revel in the thought. "Enter thou into the joy of thy Lord, of thy Lord," he repeated again and again; then turning it into a prayer, and stretching out his hands, he said, "Let me enter now, enter now, into the joy of my Lord, the joy of my Lord."

He had feared lest in his weakness and suffering some impatient word should escape him, and he should thus dishonour his Lord. He had begged his dear wife to put it down to nature's weakness, but her prediction was verified. The Lord's grace was all sufficient. No murmuring or impatient word passed his lips. While his deep gratitude and affection for the smallest service rendered him were touching and beautiful to see, and every one felt it a privilege to wait upon him.

And thus the hours passed, he fighting the last battle; his dear wife, worn with many watchings, wearied out physically but wonderfully supported in spirit, with words of faith and hope cheering him as he breasted the billows, and watching for his release.

Prayers from many loving hearts in England, China, and France, were being answered that night. There could be no doubt about it. And the word the memory of that scene calls up spontaneously to my mind is "Mahanaim," for that chamber of death was then the rendezvous of the hosts of God.

The memory of that scene calls up spontaneously to my mind is "Mahanaim," for that chamber of death was then the rendezvous of the hosts of God.

It was six in the morning. Nature outside was awaking in the first fresh joy of morning light. The sun had risen in a sky of cloudless blue. The birds were singing their morning song just outside the slightly opened window, while the carillon of the Easter bells came sounding joyously through the air.

Within, we were standing on the borderland, close by the gates which were opening to another who, having fought the good fight through Christ, was more than conqueror.

The change had come, the contracted features and glazing eyes told that the last struggle was entered on. A hurried "He is going" escaped us. I did not expect to hear him speak again, and, as consciousness seemed fading, I said, "The Master is come, and calleth for thee." He took it in, and to my surprise, with a last effort, said, "Then lift me up, that I may give another note of praise." Putting my arms around him, I drew him gently forward. Then as fast as his poor breath came, he turned it into praise. "Praise the Lord, bless His holy name," he repeated again and again.

It was wonderful to listen to, and I could not help saying to the dear companion of his life and labours, who on her knees, with only half-suppressed cries from the pangs which were rending her own heart, was holding his hands and watching the shadows of death as they passed over his face, "This is a precious legacy he is leaving you."

They were like words of triumph coming out of the very realms of death. "Do you know me, precious one?"' she asked. "Know you, Gracie? It would be strange if I didn't know you," was the reply.

Then with a strength that surprised me, he added, "We have rallied together around that dish of fruit" - one of their last conversations had been about the fruit of the Tree of Life - "many a time, and the King in His beauty was there.

Farewell, Gracie; don't speak to me again, I am going to see the King!"

Those were hallowed moments. The directress and another of the sisters had joined us. Most tenderly and faithfully had they done "what they could" for him.

M. Louis, the manservant, was helping me to support him; while before him, kneeling, was she from whom the desire of her eyes was being taken.

Our tears were flowing fast, though we hardly knew why. He was looking on things which to us were invisible, and hearing sounds our dull ears could not catch. We could hear him say in a low whisper, "Come, Lord Jesus - Lord, take my spirit," then he said, "Coming, coming - come, come." With these last words our beloved brother, George Stott, went in to see the King in His beauty, on Easter morning, at half-past six.

Our tears were flowing fast, though we hardly knew why. Mr. Stott was looking on things which to us were invisible, and hearing sounds our dull ears could not catch. We could hear him say in a low whisper, "Come, Lord Jesus - Lord, take my spirit,"

Nature's pent-up grief broke forth in brief cries and sobs, but they were happy tears. “I don't mourn for him,” said his dear wife, “I mourn for myself. He is happy - he is at rest now.”

And so we knelt together to praise Him who had given us that night to see that death has no sting, and the grave no victory. “As then,” says Athanasius, “it is possible to see with the eyes that these things are true, so when death is mocked and despised by the believers in Christ, let him no longer doubt, let no one be wanting in faith that by Christ death was brought to naught and its corruption destroyed and put an end to.”

Having seen with our eyes, we set the seal of truth to this testimony.

We buried him yesterday in the Cannes cemetery. The Rev. P. W. Minto conducted the service. A number of Christian friends were present. All who knew him loved him as a true man of God, and a faithful servant of Christ. Among those present was Mr. W. T. Berger, his lifelong friend, from whose house, twenty-four years ago, he had started for the scene of his life's labour in distant China. In a few brief but beautifully appropriate words, Mr. Berger spoke of the zeal and love which had animated him in his work for Christ. He addressed words of loving sympathy and consolation to the widow, and reminded us all, for each of us the day was hastening to its close, and that we should work ‘ere the night cometh.

Then we laid him to rest, singing over his grave the Christian's 'Good Night':

“*Sleep on, beloved, sleep and take thy rest;*

Lay down thy head upon thy Saviour's breast;

We love thee well, but Jesus loves thee best.

Good-night! Good-night! Good-night!

Until the Easler glory lights the skies,

Until the dead in Jesus Christ arise,

And He shall come, but not in lowly guise.

Good-night!"

There we left the body, sleeping in joyful hope of the resurrection, "till the day dawn and the shadows flee away."

I remain, dear Mr. Broomhall, with Christian love,

Yours sincerely,

H. WEBBER.

CHAPTER 13

LETTERS

"The memory of the just is blessed." Proverbs 10:7

Another testimony must be given, for it comes from one whose kindness ought to be mentioned as an example for the imitation of others.

DEAR MR. BROOMHALL,

My acquaintance with our dear departed friend, Mr. Stott, began in, I think, the year 1868. My brother-in-law had convened at his house a meeting of friends who were interested in foreign missionary work. There was a good attendance, and it was agreed that each one present should put themselves in communication with some labourer in the foreign field, and that later on another meeting should be held, when replies received should be read. I cannot help thinking such a plan, if more often adopted, would be the means not only of bringing refreshment to our fellow-labourers in the regions beyond, but would also enable those at home more definitely and intelligently to remember them at the throne of grace.

I was unable to attend the meeting to which I refer, until just at the close, when I found that the name of Mr. George Stott, of Wenzhou, whom I had never seen and whose name in connection with the newly formed China inland Mission, I barely knew, was allotted to me.

I at once wrote, and was very gratified in due course to receive an appreciative reply.

I regret a second meeting was never held and, so far as I know, none present at the first continued their correspondence. But Mr. Stott and I regularly wrote to each other for nine years, when it was my privilege personally to become acquainted with him and Mrs. Stott on their visit to England.

The correspondence continued without interruption ever after, and it was a great pleasure to receive them into our home, although he was in such a weak state when they arrived from China, via the U.S.A., eighteen months ago.

I cannot tell you the blessing this long friendship has been to me; and the pleasure of the service, which many might easily undertake and maintain, is one I would willingly commend to others. The insight which dear Mr. Stott's letters have given me into his patient self-denying labours (which by God's blessing have been attended with so much success) have taught me many lessons which I trust never to forget, and my earnest desire for myself and all who have known and loved him, is that we may by grace be enabled to follow him as he followed Christ (1 Cor 11:1).

Our sorrow is not without hope, and the thought of our own loss is out-weighed by the contemplation of his great gain, who has now been called to enter into the joy of his Lord.

Believe me, my dear Mr. Broomhall,

Yours faithfully,

JOHN F. ALLEN.

Mr. Broomhall responds,

It is not a little remarkable that one who had to do with Mr. Stott's going out to China in 1865, who had been his faithful friend and correspondent all through his missionary life, should be residing at the place of his death and have the opportunity at his graveside to bear testimony, such as from fulness of knowledge but few others could bear, to the faithful service of his life; but this was Mr. Berger's privilege, and that which was the peculiar privilege of the living was the special and deserved honour of our departed brother.

Mr. Berger wrote as follows:-

VILLA TALBOT, CANNES,

April 23, 1889.

"DEAR MR. BROOMHALL,

Who can estimate the issue of a single grain of wheat falling into the ground and dying? Many lives will surely spring up there from and in consequence thereof.

It has pleased God to take to Himself His faithful servant, George Stott; late of Wenzhou, China, than whom it would be difficult to find one more devoted and steadfast in prosecuting the work he believed the Lord had given him to do.

We committed his remains to the tomb yesterday afternoon, to await the voice of the Son of God calling those who shall hear it (His sleeping saints) to come forth from their graves, that they with the changed living ones may together ascend to meet and be with the Lord forever.

We committed his remains to the tomb to await the voice of the Son of God calling those who shall hear it (His sleeping saints) to come forth from their graves, that they with the changed living ones may together ascend to meet and be with the Lord forever.

We have reason to believe that Mr. Stott's twenty-three years' labour in China has been greatly owned and blessed. He having left in existence in Wenzhou and its neighbourhood (where, if I mistake not, no foreign missionary had previously laboured) three native churches, numbering in all about three hundred members besides as many attendants, to say nothing of the schools he inaugurated.

You will pardon my entering thus into details, when I tell you that I made Mr. Stott's acquaintance prior to his going to China in the year 1865, he being one of the five who went out when the China Inland Mission was but in its incipient state. His works do follow him. In thus writing, we do not glory in George Stott, but in the Lord, who wrought the works by His servant.

Of his devoted wife I must abstain from writing, but ask that much prayer may ascend to God on her behalf. Her heart seems set on returning to China to carry on the work she left as far as it may be in her power to do so. After twenty-three years' correspondence with Mr. and Mrs. Stott, I look back with the most pleasing remembrance of the same, and rejoice if in any measure I can be considered as having had partnership in their labours.

I remain, dear Mr. Broomhall,

Faithfully yours,

W. T. BERGER.

A lady who had spent the winter at the Asile, and had thus become acquainted with Mr. Stott, now herself in the presence of the King, wrote,

ASILE EVANGELIQUE,

ROUTE DE GRASSE, CANNES,

April 25, 1889.

DEAR SIR,

As one who had the privilege of spending this winter with Mr. Stott at the Asile, I feel I should like to send a few lines to tell you how bright a memory he has left behind with us of faith and patience and cheerful acquiescence in God's will. Indeed, that will was evidently his delight, whether it meant doing or suffering.

When speaking about plans for the future soon after he came, he said "if it were the Lord's will he would like either China or heaven.

> ***When speaking about plans for the future soon, Mr. Stottt said "if it were the Lord's will he would like either China or heaven***

We were struck with the way in which he entered into and enjoyed everything, notwithstanding his weary nights, always spent sitting up in his chair; and his graphic descriptions of his life and work in China (work so dear to him) were an unfailing source of interest. He was quite the life of our little party here, until extreme weakness and suffering made speaking too great a fatigue.

I was prevented by illness from engaging with him for some little time, and when able to see him again found a great change for the worse had taken place. Dropsy had then set in, and, after a consultation, the doctors gave no prospect of recovery or of his being able to return to China. He took this decision calmly and cheerfully, comforting his dear wife with "Nevermind, dear; nothing can really hurt us, you know."

One day, when I spoke of the discomfort his swollen leg must cause him, he said, "Oh, it is all quite right, my mind is kept continually in peace night and day, and as far as I know myself, I can say I am ready at any moment the Lord shall call me."

Several weeks of great suffering and weakness followed, borne with such Christian courage and patience as we can never forget. Sick people in the house were enabled to bear their burdens more cheerfully on hearing of him and servants and all who had to do with him, spoke of the wonderful way in which he bore his illness. There was not an approach to a murmur in his most painful moments, and always a word of welcome to those who entered his room. His gratitude for the least service or attention was very touching. He was loved by all.

The Friday before his death, I went in to see him for a few minutes. He said, "I am getting very near the kingdom now," and then as I took leave of him, “God bless you; perhaps the next time we meet will be in glory.”

The following evening we knew that the last struggle had begun; but even during that Saturday night he was full of praise to God, and was able to rise in a remarkable way above the bodily distress. “It is only the poor body that suffers,” he said, to those who were watching, “my mind is full of peace and joy.”

"Almost his last breath was spent in praising God. He asked to be raised up a little in his chair, saying, “I want to sound one more note of praise,” and then began, “Bless the Lord, O my soul,” and shortly afterwards he said, “Coming, coming, come,” and fell asleep in Jesus.

"It seemed, that Sunday morning, as if the gates of the heavenly city had been thrown open so wide to receive him, that we, too, had a foretaste of its peace and joy.

We sorrow with dear Mrs. Stott in her great loss, and pray that the Lord may be very near her in her loneliness, and that He will strengthen her to carry on the work for Him in China, which she loves so well, for the little while until they meet again in His presence. For us, amongst whom they have been this winter, their sojourn will be a precious remembrance of God's power to sustain, strengthen, and cheer in the time of trial.

Believe me, dear sir,

Yours sincerely,

ELEANOR H. MOOR.

Miss E. R. Teage writes,

It is so blessed to think of our dear friend at rest. What a “resurrection morning” it must have been for him! But one feels a great blank left. He endeared himself to all who knew him by his patient, bright spirit.

You will, I know, feel much the loss of dear Mr. Stott from your Mission. He was such a faithful and earnest worker, and has been one with you from the earliest days of the Mission. We feel so thankful to the Lord for giving us the honour of having him under our roof. He was such an example of real, childlike faith, and so happy. . .

We desire to add our testimony to that of many others in bearing witness to the blessed influence he had over those among whom he stayed during the past eighteen months, since his return to England.

Days and nights of weariness and suffering were appointed to him, and although for nearly two years he had been unable, owing to the difficulty of breathing, to lie down and take a night's rest, yet his bright spirit and childlike confidence in all the will of God concerning him seemed never to have been clouded for a moment.

His heart's desire was to return to the people among whom he laboured for more than twenty years, and greatly will he be missed by those dear native Christians, to so many of whom he was made the honoured instrument in leading them to the Saviour.

He has now been called to "rest from his labours," but we may truly say, "his works do follow him"; for the little church in the far-off heathen land, which through God's blessing is the result of years of patient toil and tested faith, stands as a living witness to the grace and love of God in using "a poor weak instrument" (as he himself would often say) to His glory.

It was at about the age of eighteen that, owing to an accident, he was obliged to undergo the amputation of one leg, and soon after this time of affliction he was led to rejoice in Jesus as his Saviour.

He then gave himself to the Lord for service, and was one of the first who went out with the China Inland Mission, to live among the people for whom he has since laboured so earnestly. His testimony to the end has been very bright; for, though suffering and extreme weakness have increased day by day, his spirit has been rejoicing in his Saviour, and his soul full of trust.

"Faint, yet pursuing" was the message he sent not many days since to some friends, and again, only four days ago, he said: "I cannot speak, cannot sing, cannot pray, can hardly think, but Jesus is my all in all." And now the race is run, and he has heard the welcome call, "Enter thou into the joy of thy Lord." In closing, we would add a verse of one of his favourite hymns as being so appropriate to his last moments:

"For me be it Christ, be it Christ hence to live.

If Jordan above me shall roll, No pang shall be mine, for in death, as in life,

Thou wilt whisper Thy peace to my soul.

It is well, it is well, with my soul."

I also append two letters written by his former school-boys, which show more than any words of mine how much he was loved and honoured.

Translation of *a Letter written by Tsiu-die-ching.*

Our pastor, Mr. Stott, came to Wenzhou twenty-four years ago to preach the gospel of Christ. At that time the good news had not yet been heard in Wenzhou and the Light of God had not then shone upon the people. No one knew where they came from, nor where they would go to after death; all men were dark and without understanding. Buddhism and Taoism had spread all over the place, and men worshipped only the gods they could see.

Seeing this, Mr. Stott's heart was pierced as with a knife. In private he laboured in prayer that the Good News of the Gospel might spread far and near, nor did he begrudge time or money. For this end he opened schools, calling in the children of the poor to learn to read about God. Morning and evening he himself taught them from the Word of God, to know that they had souls which would never die. He told them also that they had sin, that sinners could not enter the kingdom of heaven; also that God loved them and sent His Son into the world to save sinners.

Preaching the Gospel then was not easy, for when Mr. Stott first came to Wenzhou he did not understand the dialect, and had only a Ningbo man to help him rent a house and chapel. In the morning he taught the boys he had gathered into the school, and in the afternoon he preached in the chapel; this he did every day.

One morning early I remember a rowdy named Ah-doa came to the gate, and, battering it with stones, demanded entrance. Mr. Stott, asking him what he wanted, he answered: "I want to sport inside" (aimlessly amuse). He was told to come in the afternoon. He replied: "I must get in now."

Mr. Stott went out to exhort him, when Ah-doa threw a stone, and had not Mr. Stott put his head a little on one side, it must have felled him to the ground.

Many were the dangers and trials he passed through, willing to bear all if only souls were saved. I was the first boy in school, and learned there for five years, and afterwards, through the grace of God, became a preacher.

When I first entered the school Mrs. Stott had not yet come to Wenzhou, and Mr. Stott suffered much during the winter from neuralgia in his leg, but as soon as the pain was gone he was out preaching again.

Seventeen years ago he opened a chapel at Bing-yie, but as soon as opened, the people gathered in crowds and tried to start a riot to drive out the foreigner, forbidding him to preach. They did not know that Jesus would get the victory; for now there are over one hundred Christians in that place, and altogether in and around Wenzhou there are now over three hundred converts.

A little over two years after Mr. Stott came to Wenzhou, Mrs. Stott arrived, and began work among the women and girls. As soon as there were converts she instructed them in the Word of God, and taught them how to help others, forming them into a missionary band.

I remember six years ago that the Wenzhou chapel and house and school were burnt down by a riotous mob. All the foreigners were driven from the city, and the disciples scattered; but only a few weeks had gone by when Mr. Stott returned, and began to rebuild, and during the five months the buildings were being erected, our pastor had too much to do in attending to all the work himself. Then they had to live in the new house before it was quite dry, and thus, alas! He caught disease of the lungs.

Three years ago Mr. and Mrs. Stott left for England, hoping to return shortly, but the disease which took our pastor to heaven only developed. For two years he suffered without complaint, glorifying God, then joyfully ascended to heaven.

Mrs. Stott has returned to Wenzhou, remembering that the sheep were without a shepherd. She would not leave nor forsake the disciples, and seeing some of them blind, poor, and old, she has opened homes to receive such that they might not suffer cold and hunger in their helpless state.

Seeing that Mr. and Mrs. Stott have so earnestly done the will of God and kept all His commandments, their future reward must be great indeed.

Translation of a Letter written by Lui-sie-kwai.

I wish to write a few lines about our pastor, named Mr. Stott.

His native place was Scotland, where he was educated. He was sent out to China by the China Inland Mission to preach the Gospel.

His disposition was straight, and righteous, and very intelligent. In that respect there are few men like him. To look upon him was to feel awe, but to know and come near him he was gentle and gracious. In all matters he thought all round first, and then acted. His words were few, but his wisdom was great. Whatever he said he always did. His power and influence were felt by all.

He might well be called the pillar of the church at Wenzhou, for every one aimed and desired to be like him. Our pastor for many years gave himself to teaching and instructing. He loved much to go out and preach the Gospel to others.

He came to Wenzhou twenty-four years ago, and two years later Mrs. Stott joined him. Together they worked the will of God, happy that they were chosen for such work, leaving friends and relations and native country for distant Wenzhou, learning our native dialect so that they might understand our language. They organised churches, opened and maintained boarding - schools, not regarding time nor money, receiving orphans and other poor children, teaching them to read and understand the Bible. Not afraid of toil and suffering, he went out to near and distant places preaching, selling books, and helping the distressed.

All this he did that the Gospel might spread abroad.

Alas! The district of Wenzhou is given up to the worship of idols more than many other places; learned and unlearned alike worship idols. Mr. Stott seeing things in this condition, his heart was stirred up like a fire. He prayed, with sorrow and distress, that God would look down and pity the people.

Soon God gave the answer, and the Gospel spread to different places.

Three churches were formed at Wenzhou, Bing-yang, and Dong-ling. At each chapel there was a native preacher. Our pastor was not afraid of toil; every month he went himself to those stations preaching, teaching, and examining converts.

In all this work Mrs. Stott was his helper, she also teaching and instructing women and girls; and when souls were saved she taught them how to help others, and formed a 'Native Women's Missionary Band,' caring for the helpless and sorrowful, the cold and the hungry. All that was good connected with the church they earnestly and devotedly attended to, spending their whole strength in the work. For many years they thus worked, and are the foundation of the church. Now there are over three hundred converts.

Is this not good?

In 1887, Mr. and Mrs. Stott returned to their native land to visit once more their relations and friends. They had only gone a few months when Mr. Stott developed disease of the lungs.

The best doctors in medicine were called in and used, but it was God's will to call him home, and after nearly two years of suffering he fell asleep, joyfully entering the happy land.

When the news reached Wenzhou, the church members wept bitter tears. Our hearts were heavy and sad; but, reflecting on our pastor's virtues, old and young gave grateful thanks for his grace in teaching them.

All who knew and received this grace feel deeply that they are separated from him, and are very sad. Thinking of the words and actions of our beloved pastor, I cannot tell nearly all his goodness, but send these few lines.

Let those who read not despise the simplicity of my words.

The above was sent to the Chinese Christian paper for publication.

CONCLUSION

It has been said, "God buries His workers, but carries on His work." God can do without us, but He does not, and it is still true that "through the foolishness of preaching" He saves men.

Who will be His ambassadors, and carry His message even to the uttermost parts of the earth? The dark places of the earth are still full of the habitations of cruelty; and yet the missionary's life is one of surpassing joy, for who has ever tasted a delight more intense than that of seeing souls born into the kingdom, and perhaps no country has given larger results for the amount of labour bestowed than China.

It is true that as a nation the people can be dirty, treacherous, and in many instances cruel; but while they have these and other unlovely national characteristics, I can bear testimony to a warmth of devotion, fidelity, and patient endurance, not exceeded by any country, not even by our own beloved England; and I still hope to spend my remaining years in their midst, though much of the burden and responsibility must henceforth rest upon younger shoulders.

And now my story is ended, many incidents have been forgotten, others too sacred for the public eye necessarily omitted; but if what has been written of the joys and sorrows, encouragements and disappointments, of a missionary's life, will serve to cheer some lonely heart and strengthen some feeble knees that are apt to be weary through the difficulties of the way, by reminding them afresh of the Lord's own promise, "In due season ye shall reap if ye faint not," my effort will not have been in vain.

Back to Jerusalem

Supporting the underground church of China and publishing writings that have been made illegal in closed countries

www.backtojerusalem.com

Printed in Great Britain
by Amazon